1995

Forest Hills Diary

Forest Hills Diary

THE CRISIS OF LOW-INCOME HOUSING

Mario Matthew Cuomo

WITH A PREFACE BY JIMMY BRESLIN

VINTAGE BOOKS

A DIVISION OF RANDOM HOUSE

NEW YORK

First Vintage Books Edition, August 1983
Copyright © 1974 by Mario Matthew Cuomo
Preface Copyright © 1974 by Jimmy Breslin
All rights reserved under International and Pan-American
Copyright Conventions. Published in the United States by
Random House, Inc., New York, and simultaneously in Canada
by Random House of Canada Limited, Toronto. Originally
published by Random House, Inc. in 1974.

Library of Congress Cataloging in Publication Data
Cuomo, Mario Matthew.
Forest Hills diary.
1. Public housing—New York (N.Y.)—Case studies.
2. Social conflict—New York (N.Y.)—Case studies.
3. Forest Hills (New York, N.Y.)
I. Title.
HD7288.78.U52N73 1983   363.5′8   83-48042
ISBN 0-394-72173-X

Manufactured in the United States of America

Cover photograph courtesy of UPI

Preface

by Jimmy Breslin

On the high floors of the concrete skeletons, workmen call out to each other as they start work in the black cold night; it is six o'clock in the morning, but there is no dawn in New York anymore. The President in Washington has tried to save his life by changing the hours of the day. Treat cancer of the thorax with Brioschi. So the workingmen build their building in the darkness. It is not until midday, in suggested sunlight, that the buildings being built are there to see. The framework of three apartment houses climbs out of the icy ground to stand twelve stories in the sky. Guide ropes are strung around the open floors like the ropes of boxing rings to keep the metal lather from falling out of the ring. Fixed to the two strands of guide ropes are many small yellow ribbons. The yellow ribbons dance in the wind to tell the metal lather on the tenth floor where the sky around him on all sides suddenly becomes the sky under his feet.

Some day soon, in a year probably—a year is not very much time when you are dealing with three apartment houses of twelve stories each—some day soon these buildings will be finished. The last worker will swing the last hammer. An official, a doctor spanking a baby to begin life, will push open the doors to the buildings and people will go into the buildings as tenants. And the three apartment houses in Forest Hills, in the Borough of Queens, in New York City, will be at once a part of our housing statistics and a test of our worth as people. Not of our ability to build buildings. Everywhere in the world they marvel at the way Americans build high buildings. Build them quicker and at far less cost than anybody else can. Build them far safer than anybody else anywhere in the world. The test of Forest Hills will be that of the ability and will and strength of our souls, and it is here that there is much doubt and even the beginnings of despair.

For these three buildings we speak of were designed originally as an attack on the center, the heart, of the great problem that the nation faces and cannot handle: poverty and race. The original idea was to build three buildings of twenty-four stories each, build them in a middle-class area, and place in them the poor and the blacks.

The term is "scatter-site housing." The start of the beginning of breaking up the ghettos and having the poor and the blacks desegregated. Wonderful thought! Except that this scatter-site housing was to be placed in the middle of a place in New York City, in the Borough of Queens, in the neighborhood called Forest Hills. And Queens is a place that is across the river from Manhattan, and the distance is much more than that. People in Queens, when going to Manhattan, say, "I'm goin' to New York." Queens is white and it votes for Nixon and Buckley. Bella Abzug is New York? Come over to Queens, population about two million, and see.

And now the neighborhood. Forest Hills. It sounds like a place of beauty. It is mainly a cluster of apartment houses sitting alongside the noise, fumes and chaos of the Long Island Expressway. The people in the apartment houses are primarily Jewish, of Eastern European descent, who had left the Bronx and Brooklyn to get away from the crush of the blacks and the poor. Now, paying high rents, barely able to pay them, they found officialdom moving the Bronx and Brooklyn alongside them!

The city planners did not consider this while dreaming. The federal funds necessary to build the housing created more difficulty. The people of Forest Hills screamed. The politicians pandered. In deep trouble—bewildered really—John Lindsay's City Hall turned to the one person in the city they felt had the temperament to work out a solution. His name was Mario Cuomo and he was a lawyer.

"You could have a great future," a friend, after reading of the appointment, said to Cuomo.

"Yes, selling scatter-site housing," Cuomo said.

Scatter-site housing. Preach it from the pulpit on Sunday morning. Speak of it from a lectern at Yale or Berkeley. Advocate it to old classmates over coffee at Gracie Mansion. But don't take the subject to the people because they will roar against you through meetings in the night. And if you ever dare try to build scatter-site housing, the people—ordinary people, people who have lived sedentary lives, who have never done much of anything physical in their lives—will rush into the streets and they will picket and fight policemen and throw themselves in front of trucks and attempt to attack a mayor. And from the dark recesses of the American soul, little men will appear, men you have never heard of, and they will stand in front of the crowd and harangue and the television lights will turn on them and the despair for the American soul will rise with the sound of their voices.

For outside of something involving immediate life or death, there is in this country no emotion as raw and uncontrollable as that which pumps, spurts, floods through the mind and body of a person who lives in a white area and who finds, of a sudden morning, that about to move in across from him, next to him, around him, *near* him, is the most dreaded enemy of all, the people called "them."

The impulse here, as always, is to describe "them" as being black, because white people have a color fear which is so deep, and so easily excited, that I have difficulty imagining anything stronger. However, the author of this diary, who has so much more charity and hope than I, makes a compelling, precise, detailed argument that the clash we suffer in New York is between working and nonworking people, many of the unemployed being black. Class before Color, Mr. Cuomo insists. And he is a terribly difficult man to argue with. Mr. Cuomo does not publicly weep in UN Plaza for

millions starving in Biafra and then come home and kick the black
maid because she watches too much television. Mr. Cuomo doesn't
care, if indeed he knows, what Dr. Shockley said last night at the
Yale Political Union. Mr. Cuomo is too busy too late at night
trying to reason with and persuade angry, irrational white middle-
class people so that sometime somewhere in this city a few poor
people can take up their children and leave a hovel and the life it
represents and move into a place where children can sleep at night.
And where, perhaps, their defeated parents can dream a little and
maybe even think about trying.

But the job of reasoning with the whites, or, as Cuomo would
say, with the middle class (whether white or black), throwing a
shoulder into their fear so you can get something done, is so hard,
so tiring, that only a few have the ability to handle it.

On a recent cold night I attended a meeting of the local school
board in the Forest Hills district that Cuomo writes about in this
book. To the people of a place like Queens, the borough that
includes Forest Hills, "government" does not mean City Hall or
Washington. It means the schools. A true crisis in government is
not Nixon in Watergate. It is Sonny Liston in your daughter's class.
And at this school-board meeting, a woman stood in the hallway
outside the crowded auditorium smoking a cigarette and going over
the agenda. Point number six said, "The following are several
resolutions which represent possible plans or options for the zoning
of children who will reside in the 108th Street Project." *Project*.
Marvelous description! All the other people—people who live
directly across a narrow street, fifteen and twenty yards away at the
most—live in buildings called The Fairview or the Oakwood House
North. But "them," they are going to live in the Project.

The agenda then listed four special resolutions proposing district
schools to which the children who would be living in the Project
would be sent. I was a bit surprised at this, for directly across the
street from the new housing, again perhaps twenty yards away, is
big, bright Public School 220. The school is underutilized at this
time, and will be even more underutilized as the Pill threatens
aspirin. I asked the woman why there should be any discussion on
the matter. One of the proposed schools was nine blocks away.

("Resolved that the first hundred pupils from the 108th Street Housing Project go to their zoned school, P.S. 220, Queens. The next 25 go to P.S. 175; the next 25 go to P.S. 206. Any additional children . . .")

She said, "Oh, it's because of our CRMD [Children of Retarded Mental Development] children. In P.S. 220 we have all these magnificent children, cerebral palsy and all, and they've come along so far, we just couldn't have them hurt by crowding in a whole lot of new children from the Project. They would take away from our CRMD children."

"How many of these CRMD children do you have in 220?" I asked.

"Oh, I don't know, I think forty of them now. Oh, God, I love them so. Do you know how they've come along? Our school has worked so hard with them. We just can't afford to have these new pupils coming in from the *Project*."

I said, "But the new housing is directly across the street—I mean, it's only a few steps from 220."

"You may not think I'm powerful or that I can get so angry, but believe me I love these children so much that I'll chain myself to the doors. God, but I'll protect our CRMD children."

"Yes, but the new children will live only a few feet away from the school. Don't you believe in neighborhood schools?"

Tears glistened in her eyes. The voice came from the bottom of her throat. Came with a throb. "Nobody is going to harm our CRMD children! Nobody! I love them. I'll do anything I have to for our CRMD children."

First, it was "No forced busing." Then it was "Stop school pairings." Then there was "Save our neighborhoods." After which they went right to the main game, "Save our neighborhood schools." But on this night, as I left the woman in the hall, I could see that we were soon going to have truth in our civic language. If they could no longer cling to "neighborhood schools" as a code, what were they going to use? "Save Our CRMD Children!" I hardly think so. Because we simply do not have enough cerebral palsy children to go around. Polio perhaps? No, Salk knocked us out of that. Once, we could have lined a whole school street with crippled kids, braces glistening in the sun. Who would have dared walk past them? But we don't have enough cripples anymore. The March of Dimes is going bankrupt. *MD!* Muscular Dystrophy! They run telethons for MD. Where are they? Where do they live? We need thousands of them to keep our schools safe. All we have is forty retarded for P.S. 220 and we need hundreds. It is clear. Pretty soon now, the white middle-class neighborhoods are going to be forced to discard all the codes. People will be left with only real words to use in their slogans: "Save Our Schools By . . . By . . . BY KEEPING THE NIGGERS OUT!"

In my time in my city I have seen incredible acts of cowardice by men in official positions who were faced with the fear and anger of white middle-class neighborhoods. I have seen some acts of bravery, but with enormous stupidity combined with the bravery, by other officials. In all cases the results have been dismal. I have seen few men able to operate in this world of middle-class whites who feel threatened. The subject matter is supposedly houses and schools and it is cloaked with arguments over building costs and federal subsidies and teacher-pupil ratios. But everything really is about race and class. The real question is whether we are ever going to be able to live together and keep turmoil at a minimum. And in my time in my city I have seen few men who had the ability to walk toward this kind of trouble, put a strong hand into it, and then with deep intelligence and compassion, but always with that strong hand, hold onto the situation and turn it slowly, painfully, skillfully, always making certain not to inflame. And, in the end, actually improve the situation. Make gentle the soul of man. Even a little. Only a few in a lifetime. One was Bobby Kennedy and he is gone.

The first time I saw Cuomo was a couple of years ago, on a Sunday, and I was trying to duck work on a novel and instead of working I fooled around with a friend of mine, Michael Capanegro, who was thinking of starting a comeback in politics. We decided to go to a meeting of homeowners in the Corona section of Queens. Some sixty-nine homes were about to be knocked down by the city to make way for a new high school. I felt it was a terrific issue for Capanegro to get into. Michael is an attorney. He could go to court for the people and perform the ultimate political act: help some people who deserved help, and also help Capanegro by getting into the newspapers.

The meeting we went to was held in a crowded headquarters of a local volunteer ambulance unit. Capanegro and I sat at a table in the front. My wife was in the back, in the audience.

"Look at this crowd," I said to Capanegro.

"Sensational," he said.

"And they don't have anybody to help them?"

"Nah, maybe some little local lawyer, but no heavyweights like us."

"You're sure? I mean, if somebody else has been working, and we're walking in here like big shots."

"Nobody that counts is here," Capanegro said.

The meeting began and Capanegro spoke and I got up and spoke and we were great. We were ready to fight for them. We made all sorts of promises and the people raised the roof with tears and applause. Then they called on this one other person to speak. Tall, with short brown hair. He had been going through a folder while Capanegro and I had performed. Now he began to talk.

"Who is this?" I asked Capanegro.

"He's the little local lawyer they were using, Mario Cuomo."

"What's he like?" I asked.

"He should be glad two heavyweights like us are coming in to take it out of his hands."

As Capanegro talked to me, something else was coming into the ear. Smooth, connected sentences. Sentences with interesting words in them. I looked up. Now the person, this Cuomo, was starting to go over the entire history of their three- or four-year fight and he was holding the audience's attention and carrying them along, one fact after the other, plainly, convincingly and beautifully. I had not heard anybody speak like this in years.

I whispered to Capanegro, "I thought you told me this was just a little local lawyer."

"I thought he was," Capanegro said.

I looked to the back of the room. My wife was looking up at me. *"Who?"*

Cuomo. Cuomo. As I sat there I remembered Congressman Hugh Carey telling me, one night in the middle of an election we both were going to lose, about somebody he had wanted to run on a ticket with. "I got a genius nobody knows about." Hughie was saying. "He's a law professor at St. John's. Brilliant sonofabitch. Mario Cuomo. I begged him to run with me. Nobody knows him. The first time they ever hear of him, they'll be right there in his hands. But I just couldn't talk him into running."

Well, here he was, in this hall in Corona. Big, sloping shoulders, alert eyes, a smile. Obviously, even at a glance, talent. And talent willing to be tortured. Corona took hundreds of hours before it was resolved.

Out of Corona came Forest Hills. And in the pages that follow, you will see more than an account of a housing controversy. You will see the size of the mind and the amount of dedication it takes for a man who lives in this time to try to get others to accept what is right. It is lonely, excruciating work. In this country we send ambassadors to Moscow and missionaries to Peru. Billy Graham saves souls in Seoul. But we have virtually nobody who can act as chargé d'affaires for the poor in the strange, violent land of the middle-class white.

It is just possible that in the City of New York, we may have one person who might be able to do it. Mario Cuomo. He is not paid by the city. Nor does he receive any official honors or even many private accolades. Mostly he has just done things like Forest Hills as personal work. And if in his work he suffers rebuffs and failure and insults, then that is fine too. He has one very bad flaw in his makeup: the silly sonofabitch actually believes.

Forest Hills, N.Y.

Contents

All government—indeed, every human benefit and enjoyment, every virtue and every prudent act—is founded on compromise . . .

—*Edmund Burke* (as quoted in the concluding note of the Report of Investigation concerning the Forest Hills Low-Income Project which recommended the Forest Hills Compromise)

All compromise was surrender and invited new demands.

—*Ralph Waldo Emerson* (as quoted in the dissenting opinion of Commissioner John Zuccotti of the City Planning Commission explaining his vote against the Forest Hills Compromise)

Forest Hills Diary

The Background

Government must build public improvements in our complex urban areas. The need for schools, hospitals, housing projects and the like is constant and escalating. But these facilities may demand a high price from the area immediately involved and that possibility often causes harsh confrontations. As available vacant land reaches the vanishing point, disputes become more common. In an area like New York City, where noncommitted open space in established communities is practically nonexistent, it is difficult and often impossible to erect any sizable communal facility without uprooting homes or businesses and altering the character of the chosen area. The protests that result can be extended and bitter. For the most part these battles are almost purely local skirmishes and are forgotten soon after the last shot is fired. A few, however, have long-range implications.

The extraordinary controversy over the proposed construction of a low-income housing project in Forest Hills, Queens, New York, reached its highest and most clamorous pitch during the winter of 1971 and the spring of 1972. Although the area immediately affected was relatively confined—perhaps a few square miles—the bitter cries of protest from Forest Hills were heard across the nation. The issues touched a number of sensitive nerves that quickly transmitted the pain to various areas of the body politic. It was interpreted by many as a fight between whites and blacks, and more specifically between the Jew and the black. Planners and sociologists saw it as a critical commentary on this nation's crippled low-income housing policy. Urbanologists read it as a test of city governments' ability to deal with what have become commonplace traumas in urban life. Still others interpreted it as the defiant voice of an aroused middle class which, frustrated by its own growing problems, could no longer tolerate the demands being made upon it by the so-called disadvantaged.

Whatever else might be said about it, no one at all familiar with the facts would deny that the Forest Hills situation is worth studying. It is for that reason that the chronological notes set forth in this diary have been made public. In fact, these notes were never intended to be an in-depth study of the situation nor a careful appraisal of its numerous and complex implications. They were originally put down in order to supply a working, bare-bones record of the unique deliberative process in which the writer, by an extraordinary combination of circumstances, found himself engaged. Since they were personal, they took a great deal for granted, including the entire history of the related battle by a neighboring community in Corona, Queens, to save itself from obliteration as a sacrifice to a new high school. The Forest Hills and Corona disputes were inextricably intertwined. In attempting to interpret the Forest Hills situation it would, therefore, help to know at least the outlines of the Corona affair and some of the underlying legal context which produced these twin convulsions in New York City's governmental process.

The poor have always been—and always will be—with us. The problem of housing them is equally inevitable. For some three decades prior to the mid-1960's, local governments, in concert with the federal establishment, stumbled through a series of low-income housing programs all poorly designed and largely ineffectual. As the number of the poor grew larger in urban concentrations like New York City, the futility of these various programs became more evident.

In the late 1950's and early 1960's a belated recognition of the sociological evil inherent in segregation finally pushed the Supreme Court of the United States into an interpretation of the Constitution which prohibited segregation in public facilities. The logical sequel was an affirmative obligation on the part of government to promote integration. The principle and the obligation had obvious application to federally funded public housing, and government responded. Various efforts were made at mixing the races through the housing program. Until the mid-1960's the approach in areas like New York City was to attempt to blend disadvantaged blacks into white areas by small so-called vest-pocket interpolations. These were moderately successful but were mere tokens. By 1965, energized by a youthful, liberal spirit and its own splendid innocence, the federal administration decided to push for integration in housing on a more substantial scale. This produced the so-called scatter-site program.

The scatter-site program was designed, in part, to move meaningful numbers of the black poor into middle-income white communities by building low-income projects in white neighborhoods. The underlying motivation was sociological; the sanction was legal. By virtue of the legal progeny of the Supreme Court's decision in *Brown v. Board of Education*,* the federal government

---

* *Brown v. Board of Education of Topeka* was decided on May 17, 1954 (347 U.S. 483). It dealt with the constitutional invalidity of the "separate but equal doctrine" in public state-supplied educational facilities. *Gautreaux v. Chicago Housing Authority* is the leading judicial authority on the question of the constitutional obligation to supply scatter-site housing. Black tenants in, and black applicants for, public housing brought suits alleging that the Chicago Housing Authority had violated their rights under the Fourteenth Amendment, claiming, in essence, that federal housing funds were being used in such a way as to locate public housing projects in areas that were predominantly black, thereby denying the plaintiffs of their constitutional right to be protected against racial segregation. The ensuing litigation has had a long and complex history, but in essence it has been held that the Chicago Housing Authority shall provide public housing units outside of areas of racial concentration. The practical result of this is to require that some public housing, which will be occupied predominantly by black tenants, shall be located in areas that are predominantly white. (See 265 Fed. Supp. 582 (U.S. Dist. Ct., Northern Dist. Ill. 3/2/1967); 296 Fed. Supp. 907 (U.S. Dist. Ct. Northern Dist. Ill. 2/10/1969); 304 Fed. Supp. 736 (U.S. Dist. Ct. Northern Dist. Ill. 7/1/69); 436 Fed. Rept. 2nd 306 (Ct. of App. 7th Cir. 12/16/70).

could insist that in order for a city to qualify for any allotment of federal housing funds, it would be required to use a respectable portion of those funds in such a way as to accomplish meaningful integration. Impatient to show quick results the federal government began administratively to impose quotas. By the time John V. Lindsay became mayor in 1966, it had already been decided that as soon as possible New York City should place approximately 7,500 low-income units in white middle-class neighborhoods or risk the loss of all federal housing funds. Actually a number of the sites for these experimental projects had already been selected by the time Lindsay was sworn in. One of them was to be a parcel of property in Corona, Queens, an undistinguished and until then largely unknown area of New York's bedroom borough.

Corona was one of the disappearing vestiges of the ethnic pluralism that had helped make New York City the greatest city in the world. It was tucked away in an infrequently traveled area of the borough about a mile and a half north of the Long Island Expressway. Unless one was looking up relatives or searching for a really authentic Italian-American pastry shop, the chances of passing through the villagelike Corona were minimal. It was an old neighborhood; any home less than twenty years old stood out as a recent development. Some of the houses were constructed of cinder block; most of them were frame, small and neat. Many of them had been built literally by hand by the occupants or their immigrant forebears. Practically all of them had a yard with a fig tree or a grape arbor or both. Almost everyone in Corona was Italo-American and except for the newest generation spoke Italian, with all its regional variations. There were three bocci courts where paunchy Italian grandfathers played on weekends year round and in almost

It should be noted that the Supreme Court of the United States chose not to review the questions presented in the *Gautreaux* case, although Mr. Justice William Douglas, as a sole dissenter, indicated he felt the matter was worthy of review by our highest court. (Certiorari denied, 402 U.S. 922, 9/22/71.) To date, the Supreme Court has not spoken on the precise issues. See also *Shannon v. Department of Housing and Urban Development*, 436 Fed. Rept. 2nd 809 (Ct. of App. 3rd Cir. 12/30/70) and *Otero v. N.Y. City Housing Authority*, 484 Fed. Rep. 2nd 1122 (Ct. of App. 2nd Cir. 9/12/73).

all kinds of weather. The two local Catholic churches were jammed with the women of Corona each Sunday, many of them wearing the familiar black mourning costumes out of respect for loved ones who might have died ten years before. They were nice, gentle family people. Simple, hard-working, law-abiding. A vanishing breed. Except for the local doctor and a few second-generation lawyers none had managed to move much higher economically than low middle class. The fact was they really didn't care to. Everything they needed or wanted they had in Corona. Their way of life was almost uniquely placid. By actual Police Department statistics no serious crime of violence had been recorded in this small part of Queens since 1960. Most never even considered moving. In some cases the people occupying a house had been preceded by two generations in the same structure. Family ties had been intensified by numerous neighborhood marriages, so that almost everyone could be called "cousin."

For the most part when they returned to their homes after a day's work, the Corona people left the outside world totally. There was little interest in political and social matters. The local assemblyman and state senator were nice boys from good families who had done well for themselves and for whom their vote was automatic. But when they were compelled to serve their nation in times of crisis the people of Corona had responded dramatically. At the local VFW hall—in effect the Corona community house— there was a long list of heavily voweled names of boys and men who had given their lives for their country in three wars.

The heart of Corona was perhaps a hundred houses filled with people like these. They sat clustered together about a mile south of the huge Lefrak City apartment complex which abutted on the Long Island Expressway.

Although fully constructed by 1966, Lefrak City was not yet fully occupied. Corona was the old world, Lefrak City the new. It consisted of a series of huge concrete elongated boxes in which thousands of people were crowded together disparately in apartments, to form a new conglomeration if not a new community. It had been built and named after one of the city's master builders. It had everything but a high school and its owner was desperate for one.

Diagonally across the Long Island Expressway to the south, a few hundred feet or so away, was the edge of the Forest Hills community. At one time it had been forest and hills, but no one who was less than forty years old could possibly have remembered it being so. It had long since lost its battle with the developers, so that from the Long Island Expressway south to Queens Boulevard it was now mostly apartment buildings mashed together and surrounding a few score neat, well-appointed one-family homes, many of them attached. The community was mostly Jewish with a large number of Orthodox Jews who had fled from other parts of the city to the safety of Forest Hills, where they could live together in tight groups as their religious orientation practically mandated. They were bright, energetic people who by dint of their industry and natural talents had achieved a good degree of material success. Everyone was comfortable or better. The area had one of the highest levels of education in the city. Its residents were active, generally regarded as liberally disposed—people who were concerned with sociology, politics, and government. Until late 1966 they had little to do with Corona and knew practically nothing about that community only a few miles away. They were closer in background and style to the Lefrak City citizens, but even then, the concrete border strip that made up the Long Island Expressway permitted and promoted separate existences.

On the face of it, neither Corona nor Forest Hills would have seemed to be logical receptacles for the placing of large numbers of low-income blacks, although one might have guessed that the presumably more liberal Forest Hills community would have been better disposed to the objective, if not the implementation, of a scatter-site program. Both were selected by the operation of the city's elusive—and sometimes baffling—site-selection process, about which the public at large knew little if anything. That process has not been substantially changed since 1966.

The federal government provides subsidies for low-income projects but insists that the precise area for their construction be selected by the local government involved after giving the community immediately affected its say—if not its way. As one might have assumed even in 1966, and as has now become painfully clear, the problem of selecting an area for the project can be an exquisitely difficult one. The legal and political necessity for community involvement in the choice makes the process infinitely more troublesome, however morally virtuous the insistence upon such involvement might appear to be. Surely history has shown that the benevolent despotism of Robert Moses had a much better track record for achievement. In any event, the law requires that the site-selection process for a housing project in New York City start with a so-called Plan and Project, a rough outline of a proposed development put together by the local agency in charge, the New York City Housing Authority. That Plan and Project must then be subjected to the scrutiny of the New York City Planning Commission, a group of seven individuals, all of whom are appointed by the mayor and whose task it is to devise, promote, and guard the physical planning and development of the entire city. In the statutory scheme, the City Planning Commission, after it completes its study, is required to advise and recommend to the body which makes the ultimate judgment, the Board of Estimate of the City of New York.

The Board of Estimate consists of the mayor, the president of the City Council, the New York City comptroller and the president of each of the boroughs. Each of the borough presidents casts two votes; and each of the three city-wide officials, four.

In theory, the Board of Estimate, consisting as it does of elected officials, is responsive to the felt desires of the community at large. In order to aid the Board of Estimate in properly appraising community sentiment the law calls for public hearings both before the City Planning Commission and the Board of Estimate. Several years ago, as a further small concession to the necessity for community involvement, the city created community planning boards (now simply known as Community Boards) consisting of volunteer groups, most of whom are appointed by the local borough presidents, for each of sixty-two planning districts in the City. These groups have no juridical power and depend for their effectiveness upon the discretion of the vote casters on the City

Planning Commission and Board of Estimate and their ability to threaten persuasively political retribution to those politicians who fail to be decently responsive to them. In 1966 the influence of these boards was insignificant. Partially by virtue of what has happened since then in both Forest Hills and Corona, they are today a good deal more meaningful, although still bereft of any real legal power. The Community Board is given an opportunity to present its opinion to both the City Planning Commission and the Board of Estimate in the case of any proposed low-income housing project.

The machinery for the selection of the site for a public school in the City of New York differs markedly from that prescribed for the choice of a housing project location. Neither the City Planning Commission nor the Board of Estimate decides what property will be appropriated in order to find space for a new school. That decision is made by the Site Selection Board and is implemented by the mayor.

The Site Selection Board was added to New York City's organic law as part of the major revision of the New York City charter effective in 1963. That the basic thrust of that entire charter change may have been a regrettable miscalculation is evidenced now by the predominant opinion that the direction of the city's governmental structure should be reversed and a new move made toward "decentralization." The aim of the 1963 charter revision was to create a strong central government whose principal powers would reside in the mayor as chief executive. The Site Selection Board concept was consistent with this emphasis and with the theory that the complex problems of allocation of services and the intricate judgment as to the location of community projects be moved away from the communities and into the mayor's office, where uniformity and predictability might better be served. Thus, the judgment as to site selection for projects like public schools—which is nothing less than a judgment as to which individuals and communities in the city should be called upon to offer their services for the commonweal—was moved out of the Board of Estimate and into this new board. Its design assured control by the mayor. Three of the board's five members are his appointees: the director of the budget, the chairman of the City Planning Commission and the commissioner of the Department of Real Estate. The two elected officials who sit on the board, the comptroller and the borough president of the borough immediately affected, hold only a minority position, so that on the Site Selection Board what the mayor wants the mayor gets. The board holds public hearings before announcing its decisions.

The Forest Hills problem began with the housing project scheduled for Corona. In 1966 the Housing Authority proposed a Plan and Project which described a low-income housing project that would consume four and a half acres in Corona and that would house 509 low-income tenants. The designated four and a half acres were mostly vacant; there were only four homes on the entire tract, only one of which was owner-occupied. Simultaneously, several other scatter sites were selected in various parts of the city. All of them were to find the route through the City Planning Commission and Board of Estimate dangerous; the Corona project found it impassable.

The City Planning Commission approved the project with little difficulty, but in late 1966, when it came before the Board of Estimate for a public hearing, the opposition was massive. It is not clear exactly who orchestrated the opposition or at whose instance the opponents were there, but it is clear who did not make up the opposition. It was not the people of Corona. Only two or three of the Corona people were even present at the board hearing but busloads of people from the Lefrak City area appeared and argued furiously that there was a much greater need for a high school than there was for a low-income housing project. This, and whatever other pressure was brought to bear, worked. In a last-minute move the Corona housing project was withdrawn from consideration by the Board of Estimate with the explicit representation on the part of the board that the project would be replaced by a high school and athletic field.

Had it ended there, with a simple switch of high school for housing project, there would have been a single confrontation: the Corona community against the City of New York. That struggle did eventually ensue, but so did another and fiercer one.

The city's deep commitment to the theory of scatter-site housing impelled them to replace the project lost in Corona by finding another location in the general vicinity. What the city found—with record speed—was a vacant eight-and-a-half-acre site across the Expressway on 108th Street in Forest Hills, a tract that had lain suspiciously fallow for years, notwithstanding the building boom that had chewed up the rest of the land in the area.

These twins, the school site now designated for Corona and the low-income housing project now scheduled for Forest Hills, were born of the same aborted process, and both showed the scars. Neither had been preceded by the kind of investigation, study, and deliberate judgment that the complexities of the situation deserved. The school for Corona was a product of the sudden decision to replace the housing project. That, in turn, required a second precipitous determination to compensate for the initial switch by finding a new site for the project. The planning for the school was particularly egregious. In its haste to hide the pea under the shell, the city clumsily expanded the original four-and-a-half-acre site earmarked for the project into a twelve-and-a-half-acre site in order to accommodate the school and field. The twelve and a half acres would have required the obliteration of sixty-nine homes in Corona and five of its business establishments. With one stroke it would have destroyed the heart of Corona and all that it represented as a fleshy realization of this city's historical pluralism.

The Corona plan was scheduled to be heard by the Site Selection Board at a public hearing in March of 1967.

In the meantime the city had managed somehow to have the Board of Estimate approve the low-income housing project in Forest Hills at a meeting in December 1966. That the opposition in the Board of Estimate was not more strenuous is attributable to the suddenness of the switch and the lack of adequate vehicles for communication with the community. It also indicated that the behind-the-scenes political work had been done well. The local Community Planning Board was later to complain that it had been given practically no opportunity to study and discuss the matter in the neighborhood. As events have shown, had the community been given full warning and a worthwhile opportunity to participate, the project might never have left the drawing board.

As it was, in the switch, the project had grown too. Instead of 509 apartments, there were now contemplated approximately 840.

Belatedly, in early 1967, an awareness of what was about to happen to its community finally filtered down to the citizens of Corona. Confused and frightened, they turned to their representatives and eventually were able to retain an attorney who had only recently been successful in protecting the owners of several junk yards in Willets Point, a neighboring community, from extinction at the hands of Mayor Robert Wagner and Commissioner Robert Moses. With little money and no organization other than a hastily constructed committee put together at a midnight meeting at the VFW hall, Corona set about to marshal its troops for a battle at the Site Selection Board.

In the naïve belief that the argument could be won with facts and logic, the community set about frantically to find other sites in the area that would not only be more suitable for the high school but would avoid the tragic destruction of a community. The third generation of Corona people, several teen-age girls and boys, led a fact-finding expedition which produced impressive statistics, assessed valuations, population figures, transportation data, and even income figures. Eventually, a number of alternate sites were found which appeared to meet the city's needs so clearly that it was difficult to see how they could be rejected. With their attorney, the Corona people collected, analyzed, graphed and set down in writing the information they had gathered. They lined up speakers, hired buses and on March 20, 1967, Corona was at City Hall for its opportunity to be heard before the Site Selection Board.

Corona had come to be heard, but the board had not come to listen. The so-called hearing was a travesty. Only one of the five members was present; the other four were otherwise engaged and were content to send second- and third-echelon deputies. The Board of Education of the City of New York, which desired the site, sent its representative. He dispassionately recited the formal conclusions of the city's educational officials: a site was needed;

the damage to the community would be unfortunate but inevitable; the homes and businesses should be removed as soon as possible. The community's case took hours. Their attorney argued for nearly fifty minutes. Dozens of residents and officials spoke. Their legal briefs and ponderous statistical data, including complete analyses of several alternate sites, were handed up to the board for consideration. But when the hearing ended, the solitary board member present and the four alter egos for the absent members required only five minutes of deliberation to arrive at a unanimous decision against the community—without so much as looking at the briefs and data that had been offered! In a startling display of prescience, one of the absent members had left behind a lengthy written decision explaining the vote which he had not been present to register himself, on the basis of evidence which he had not been there to hear. In an even more extraordinary display of contempt for the community's awareness, his representative read the opinion aloud to the audience, which was first dumbstruck and then enraged.

What the people of Corona had most lacked initially was a respect for political activism. They were, accordingly, easy marks. But in that one day at the Site Selection Board they learned their lesson and learned it well. Their rage and disgust with what had occurred that day fired them for a battle with the city and sustained them throughout five years of struggle that were to follow. They went from the Site Selection Board into court. The sham quality of the board hearing was so clearly evident that a second hearing at the Site Selection Board was necessarily scheduled. By then, a few months later, Corona's voice was beginning to be heard. They were able to persuade two of the members of the board, the borough president and the comptroller, that they were right, but the mayor's three designees refused to budge, so that the majority decision was in favor of condemning the Corona community.

The legal fight resumed, and before it was over there were to be dozens of court appearances and hundreds of arguments. For more than two years the city was prevented from actually taking title to the Corona properties. But by October of 1969 the legal remedies had been exhausted and the city officially condemned the Corona homes and businesses.

The Corona people had tried everything they could think of. In desperation their lawyer had constructed a compromise solution which he attempted, repeatedly, but futilely to convince the city fathers to accept or at least consider. From time to time their hopes were buoyed by the interest and sympathy of people like Fioravante Perrotta, then executive assistant to the mayor, and Frank Arricale, then chairman of the city's Department of Relocation, but even these sympathizers, for all of their efforts, were ineffectual. Now, by October 1969, it appeared as though the Corona fight was virtually over. Even if by some miracle the city could be persuaded it was wrong, the fact that an actual condemnation had now taken place would mean that in order to undo it, a special act of the legislature would have to be adopted, and that had never been done in the history of the state. What hope was left for Corona was regarded as pure fantasy.

While Corona was waging its almost pathetic battle with the city from 1967 to 1969, the Forest Hills project lay dormant. As far as the public could tell, the city had lost interest in it. Actually, the city had discovered that the subsurface of the land was so poor that extensive and costly piling would be needed. This problem drove the projected costs of curing the land up to a point which exceeded the federal subsidy guidelines. The project would simply be too expensive. Numerous redesigns were being worked on quietly and attempts were being made to increase the federal limits, but the ostensible lack of activity had lulled the Forest Hills community into a sense of security that was ultimately proven to be cruelly false. Rumors from undisclosed but "reliable" sources convinced the Forest Hills community that the project would never be built. These rumors had reached Corona, and it was natural therefore for the Corona community to suggest, as one of the alternatives to its destruction, that the high school and field be built at the Forest Hills site on the vacant land instead of in Corona. Ironically, the principal opposition to this alternative came from several Forest Hills residents who doggedly charged Corona with a selfish reluctance to make its contribution to the commonweal. A year or so later their tune was to change.

Although virtually spiritless after the condemnation in 1969, Corona's people struggled on. Necessarily, the essential part of their battle was the legal fight to stay in their homes, which now belonged to the city, for as long as possible, hoping that in the interim a miracle might occur. Perhaps Lindsay would not be reelected in 1969 and a new mayor would help them. Perhaps even if he were reelected, lightning would knock him from his horse as it did Saul; or he would see the evil of his persecution and he would rescue them. However illusory the hope, they continued to fight and managed to keep the city from evicting them.

It was during this period that Vito Battista, the fiery assemblyman from East New York, long an outspoken opponent of the Lindsay administration, came to Corona. While offering nothing new by way of argument, he brought to Corona an amazing knack for publicity gathering. The spotlight followed him wherever he went and he contrived one colorful device after another to win headlines. There were some who shrank back in embarrassment at some of his tactics, but there was no denying that they were finally successful in bringing Corona's plight to the attention of the public at large. Unfortunately, however, the administration's abiding contempt for Assemblyman Battista made him totally useless as an instrument for the mayor's conversion.

Then the miracle happened. It came in an unlikely form. Jimmy Breslin, a celebrated, controversial, and himself colorful writer, reporter, columnist, and quasi-politician came to one of Corona's innumerable meetings at the request of an old friend, Mike Capanegro who had been born and raised there. Aside from Capanegro, a well-known lawyer who had long since outgrown Corona, Breslin's only apparent connection with the people of the community was that he had an Italian wife and an affinity for Italian food. For whatever reason, it took Breslin only one night of listening to and observing the Corona people to become passionately convinced that they were right and should be helped. He began a one-man media campaign which eventually moved the liberal press of New York City—and even the *Los Angeles*

Times—to take up the cudgels for Corona. The pressure finally forced open the doors of the mayor's office in City Hall. Breslin was able to accomplish what Corona had not been able to get close to: a meeting with a mayor's representative who was willing to listen.

Two weeks later, Richard Aurelio, then deputy mayor, sat in his office in City Hall and listened to Corona's lawyer plead their case. He asked what solution if any was possible, and the first suggestion was that the school be moved to 108th Street in Forest Hills, since it appeared that the low-income housing project would never be built there. Aurelio immediately picked up a phone and spoke to the chairman of the New York City Housing Authority, Simeon Golar. Golar informed him that all problems had been resolved with respect to the Forest Hills site and that a public announcement that the project would be going forward was imminent. Aurelio was convinced by that conversation that the 108th Street project could not be moved. Corona's lawyer, left now with no other alternative, suggested a compromise whereby the high school could be built and the community saved. Basically it called for eliminating ball fields that were scheduled as part of the complex and replacing them with fields in nearby Flushing Meadow Park. This and other adjustments in the foundation lines of the school itself, together with some elaborate legal maneuvering, would leave all of the sixty-nine homes intact except fourteen, each of which could be moved to another part of the original site only a block from their original locations. Everyone recognized the numerous problems of implementation in such a plan. First of all, it would require Mayor Lindsay to state that he had made a mistake, and even if that could be accomplished, it would then require the passage of a unique Act by the State Legislature. But Aurelio, like Breslin, was convinced. Largely at his urging, the mayor agreed to the plan, and the city set about attempting to implement it.

The so-called Corona compromise was publicly announced by the mayor at a late-afternoon press conference at City Hall on December 2, 1970. The initial burst of publicity was nearly all commendatory. The plan's uniqueness and human-interest dimensions made good fodder for the media people. Late on the same day of the announcement the Corona people met at the VFW Hall to hear the plan explained. All the home owners were there, as was the whole cast of characters that had become involved, including Battista, Breslin, and even Secretary of State John Lomenzo, whom the governor had sent some months earlier as his personal representative. The plan offered the Corona home owners more than they had dreamed was possible only several weeks earlier. Battista appeared to be content at that first meeting and was duly recognized by the other speakers as a helpful if not crucial participant in the whole process that had led to the compromise. But following the meeting, as the cameras focused on the authors of the compromise and left Battista temporarily in the shadows, he began finding reasons for unhappiness. He now interpreted the mayor's concession as a sign of weakness and as an invitation to demand more. He persuaded several of the home owners, including Lilly Manasseri and Ralph Dellacona, seasoned veterans of the five-year war, that instead of acquiescence in the compromise they should oppose it vigorously on the theory that Lindsay would be forced to capitulate entirely if the pressure could be kept up. The home owners' attorney and others who were closer to the scene were convinced that compromise was as far as the mayor would go and that it would be foolhardy to give up what was won by demanding what was unobtainable. It was a legitimate and difficult difference of opinion. Issue was joined again, but now it had become an internecine dispute. The compromisers were labeled as sell-outs and worse. Battista's battlers thrived in the warmth of the television lights. Each exposure incited them to create further and more imaginative arguments, in some cases only barely restrained by the actual facts. The compromisers were painted blacker and blacker while the Battista band suggested, none too subtly, all sorts of perverse considerations that might have motivated their erstwhile lawyer to offer and promote the compromise. It was largely a one-sided battle; the supporters of the plan decided that in this instance the discretion of silence would be the better part of valor. They spent all their efforts attempting to push the legislation that was needed to implement the plan through the labyrinth of legislative bureaucracy in Albany while ducking the brick bats being flung by the irascible Vito and his followers. Assemblyman Joe Lisa and Senator Nick Ferraro led the legislative fight.

This phase of the Corona struggle was to prove even more excruciating than the first. Although the governor had promised Lisa and Ferraro his full support for the compromise plan, Battista was somehow able to frustrate it, and the legislature recessed in the early summer of 1971 without having adopted the vital legislation.

Eventually this defeat proved to be a boon because the mayor stood fast during the summer of 1971 and in fact spent that summer working out a further variation of the original plan with the Corona lawyer. The plan as revised left only four homes which would have to be relocated immediately and came even closer to total victory for the home owners.

In January 1972, the new version of the compromise plan was submitted to the Legislature and by this time Vito's influence had been calculated and offset. After an agonizing six months the Lisa-Ferraro Corona compromise bill was finally passed and signed by the governor at the eleventh hour on June 8, 1972. The feelings of the vast majority of the Corona community at that point are to some extent revealed in the final letter written by the home owners' attorney on the day after the bill was signed.

June 9, 1972

Corona Taxpayers Association
53-10 102nd Street
Corona, New York 11368

Attention: Mr. and Mrs. John Ioli

Dear John and Anne:

We have come so far that looking back now, it's difficult to see where the journey started. We've been marching for nearly six years and it looks as though we're finally back home. It's not the same home—some have left, others have been alienated—but it's still home. It can be rebuilt, refurbished and—depending on all of you—it can even become a better place to live than it was.

I think now of almost six years of struggle. How many cups of black coffee would you say? It must have been at least a thousand. How many meetings at the VFW? How many grim reports about our continuing inability to move politicians and to convince the decision-makers that we were right? How many nights when we discussed and revelled in small victories, with our hope being rekindled, and burning just high enough to sustain us through the next disappointment? And all the dramatic things that happened, starting particularly when Breslin (by whatever magic moved that curious heart and brain of his), decided to bring our story to the public, and more importantly, into the Mayor's office itself. And think too of Vito and Lilly and Ralph and how the noise they made—however obstreperous—kept us in the public's eye and eventually won its sympathy. And remember when the compromise was first announced more than a year and a half ago, following the agonizing decision to end the battle in return for a precedent-shattering agreement by the City and State to place us as nearly as possible in the status quo. The confusion, the debates, the misunderstanding, the disappointment. Think about the hundreds of phone calls, the dozens of meetings, the furious arguments, the tears, the bus trips, the parties, the pain—think about all that and realize, if you can, that now it's over.

What does it all mean? Most of us have been so busy with the actual fray that we've not paused long enough to think through what it was really all about. Sure, it involved the homes and your right to stay in them and to make your lives there. But it involved a great deal more. It involved the integrity of the whole governmental system. A mistake was made. Everyone knew it. The question was: Would the System be big enough to confess and correct its own blunder? And the System did. And it did so not because it was forced to by vast political strength—we had none of that—it did so not because of the financial power of our group—because we were all practically beggars. In the end all we had on our side was the rightness of what we were saying. And in the end it was rightness that prevailed.

Just think about it: when is the last time that happened? Isn't it good to know it *can* happen?

You may be thinking that you in Corona have paid so much in terms of anguish, frustration and permanently ingrained suspicion that it is difficult to see this outcome as a victory at all. But I think you can, and you should, think of it in its best terms and start from there in rebuilding your home. Forget the antagonisms of the past; embrace Lilly and Ralph. Join yourselves together now permanently for the future, not to fight off the enemy as you have for more than five years, but now to work constructively to help one another. This is especially needed with respect to those of you who will have to be relocated. Certainly, you have learned by now the value of staying alert and interested and involved and the importance of being active in pursuit of what you think is right. You know now that given enough perseverance and effort, the System will respond. That should be enough to sustain you.

I see it now as a time for wine and music and block parties and celebration and church. You should, in some way, come together for one night to remember the past, to relish the outcome, to plan for the future and to say "thank you." There are an awful lot of people to thank, after you have congratulated yourselves. Dozens of individuals have contributed to your victory; all of them were indispensable. Can you say that the outcome would have been the same were it not for Dick Aurelio and Mayor Lindsay's agreement to offer the compromise? Or where would we have been without Breslin and Capanegro who introduced him to us? Didn't Vito play a role? And Lomenzo, and finally the Governor himself. And before them there were Chetta, Faberrizzi, Joe Lisa Sr. and Eddie Tymon. And how about the media? There were times when we felt the media's interest in the spectacular had the effect of obscuring the truth of the Corona situation. But, on the other hand, consider the Long Island Daily Press's repeated statements of position in our support. The NEWS and the TIMES were generous in their coverage. Television and radio came to our assistance, and remember the many other political officials who did take the time and trouble to put their oar in for Corona. Have you forgotten Judges Cariello and Procaccino voting in our favor? And how hard Fred Perrotta fought for us, even at a grave risk to his own political career. How many hours did Sanford Freedman spend working with us? And what about Dick Brown and Mickey Beller?

And, of course, Joe Lisa and Nickey Ferarro whose names now will be for all time imprinted on the history-making bill which returned your homes. Poor Joe, the beating he took—the work he did!

You should say "thank you" to them not only because it is owed them, but also to inspire these people, and others like them, with the knowledge that good things are appreciated and such things will be worth doing again.

They waited until the final day to let us know our fate. The guillotine was permitted to drop to the point where one more swing would have ended us. But it's over now. The bill is signed. The battle is won, and it's time for other things.

I congratulate you. I wish you well. If I can help you, I'll be around.

Sincerely,
Mario Matthew Cuomo

Throughout the year and a half the Corona compromise was forging its way on the grueling path to realization, the Forest Hills controversy heated up. The announcement of the compromise in December 1970 again focused attention on the project at 108th Street. While the compromise signaled a victory for Corona it also announced a resumption of activity at 108th Street. Forest Hills was aroused. Assemblyman Herb Miller, who had been an opponent of the project from the beginning and who had been led to believe that it was dead, began marshaling forces. Another potential folk hero—a heavy-set, gruff, elemental businessman named Jerry Birbach who owned a home in Forest Hills—came to the fore. Disgusted with politics and politicians, he put together his own organization, the Forest Hills Residents Association, and began collecting money and support for a legal and publicity war against the project. In late 1970 Battista and his group joined with Miller and Birbach in arguing that the best answer would be to kill the project at 108th Street and to replace it with the high school, thereby leaving Corona intact and Forest Hills safe from the threat of an intrusion of a large number of low-income blacks. The argument came from Forest Hills a year or so too late, but it had great appeal in many quarters. It was enhanced by many factors: street crime was a public scandal; a middle-class revolution was brewing; Lindsay's popularity was on the wane; the cry for community control was growing louder, and the Corona compromise itself served as a source of hope to all anti-establishment forces. Forest Hills' voice was also amplified by the homogeneity of their group. They were largely, if not exclusively, Jewish, and they saw the threat to their community as a threat to Jewish survival in the city.

They were able to gather substantial sums of money and finance a vigorous legal assault. Several lawsuits were started and one was pressed to the state's highest court, the Court of Appeals. However, except for a short-lived victory in one court, the legal attack was eventually to fail. In the meantime, picketing, protest marches, and the citywide publicity grew in intensity. The pressure finally produced an act of the Legislature sponsored by State Senator Marty Knorr and Assemblyman Jack Gallagher which would have effectively killed the project, but that bill was vetoed by Governor Rockefeller in June 1972 on the ground that it was unconstitutional.

Throughout the battle, the Forest Hills opponents set their sights on Mayor Lindsay and battered him relentlessly. They followed him to Florida, where Lindsay was involved in an ill-fated presidential primary. There are some political pundits who say they were responsible in no small measure for the Lindsay debacle in that state. But the mayor and Simeon Golar, chairman of the Housing Authority, who was also being regularly assaulted by Forest Hills' rhetoric, stood fast and moved ahead with their plans for three 24-story low-income high-rise buildings housing 842 tenants at the 108th Street site.

When the work on the foundation actually began at the site, the pressure grew still greater. Politically, there was no doubt the situation was the single most irksome embarrassment to the Lindsay administration. But it was more than that: it was now an undeniably dangerous situation. The dispute was being interpreted as a battle between the Jews and the blacks. In a time of growing middle-class discontent the increasing polarization was a serious problem. There were even threats of violence. There was no indication that the community could be made to accept the project as planned, and the protests from Forest Hills became louder and more anguished. The dangers could not be ignored. The mayor determined something had to be done. He decided to reach beyond government to some independent source to serve as a fact-finder or mediator. He was not sure precisely how the effort should be structured, or whether it would have any reasonable chance for success, but for whatever it might be worth, he decided in May of 1972 to try it.

The Diary

Former Deputy Mayor Dick Aurelio called me yesterday to talk about the situation in Forest Hills. He talked generally at first—about the mayor's concern that the embittered Forest Hills community might boil over, the increasing racial polarization, and the threat it posed to the city's housing program. Eventually he got around to the possibility of using some sort of independent fact-finder, and then finally asked me whether I'd be willing to do it for the city. He was frank—it was a long shot and there would probably not be anything in it for me but a great deal of aggravation. But he wanted me to try it. Apparently, some months ago the idea had been suggested to Ted Kheel and Basil Patterson on the theory that communication lines had broken down between the mayor and the community and something dramatic was needed. Rumor has it that they both turned down the "opportunity" after deciding that for various reasons it would not be feasible.

Something like this was fairly predictable. The situation has been a mess for a long time and its unhappy implications with respect to racial tensions eventually had to call for some kind of mediation or reconciliation. But I was surprised that the mayor's office would think of me, notwithstanding our success in working out a resolution of the Corona situation, which we had fought over for more than five years. The undertaking would be such a sensitive one, I would have thought the mayor would want somebody more predictably in tune with his own thinking. In any event, after a half hour or so, I told Dick I would consider trying it provided it was understood I would in fact be an independent agent and not merely a vehicle for presenting some prearranged plan. I also wanted some assurances of receptivity on the part of the warring factions.

It was left at that and I shunted the matter to the back of my mind. There were many pressing obligations in the office and I really didn't expect anything tangible to materialize—at least for a while. Dick's low-key manner gave me the impression it was something that would take time to work out.

When I finished the oral argument against Charlie Moerdler in the Lefrak case this morning, there was nothing further from my mind than my conversation with Aurelio. We had just completed a critical and exhausting session in the Appellate Division, and by the time I got back to the office I was ready for a cup of coffee and a good look out my window. Instead, I was greeted by an excited message from our switchboard operator that the mayor's office was looking for me and it was "urgent." I called back and the mayor got on the phone. The conversation was simple enough. The mayor asked if I would agree to be the "independent agent." I was hardly prepared to answer him; I had given the matter practically no thought since yesterday, but for some reason he thought time was of the essence, so I had only an hour or so to think it through and get back to him. Maybe that was a blessing—I'm inclined to think that the proposal and the choice were so complex and troublesome that they could have been analyzed indefinitely—and painfully. Necessity can make things easier sometimes, and it did today. There wasn't enough time to do more than work from a hastily reinforced instinct. And instinct spoke quite clearly: "The problem is a serious one with enormous implications, most of them bad. It can't make it worse if you're involved and it might—just might—be helpful. Maybe just displaying the facts and various positions objectively and clearly and without foggy rhetoric will help." I called the mayor back and agreed to do it, asking only the assurance of independence and some initial receptivity. The mayor called later in the day to say that he and others on his staff had called most of the principals and the suggestion had been fairly well received.

There was no time for detailed planning; the release was going out today from his office. They read it to me quickly. While I was not clear as to the need for such urgency, it was plain they felt it had to be done as soon as possible for reasons they preferred not to go into. "O.K., let it go." Did I want to come to City Hall tonight? "No." There was something I had to do. I did it. I had two cups of coffee and a long, long look out my window toward New Jersey.*

It had happened so quickly there was practically no impact at first. It was like dislocating a finger in a ball game; you don't really feel it until the action has stopped and you're on the bench. I thought about the staggering complexity of the problem; it was even worse than Corona. I thought about the problems it would present at the office—and elsewhere. I even thought about my reasons for saying "yes" and that got very complicated. In the end it was easier simply to accept the fact that it was done, the commitment was made, and to start thinking about how to handle it.

Thursday, May 18, 1972

We met at the mayor's office in City Hall at 10 A.M. this morning. We were late starting because Professor Walter Sayre, who had been in with his Honor, collapsed and later died of a heart attack.

By the time the mayor was ready to see me my perspective was in good shape; lightning striking Professor Sayre had seen to that. I think it had the same effect on the mayor. We talked alone for a few minutes without even mentioning Forest Hills—it *is* a hard life, and a short one.

---

* The office is located on the nineteenth floor of 32 Court Street in Brooklyn and the windows look out, westerly, over the Bay, Governors Island, Liberty Island, Ellis Island and all that's beyond.

The mayor had received what he called good feedback. Everybody was sick of the situation and eager to make the most of any opportunity to end it sanely. Did I need anything? How could he help? I wasn't ready to say yet. The whole thing had been launched with very little detail—the only authority I received was spelled out tersely in the few lines of the mayor's release: Cuomo was to be a fact-finder who would report back to the mayor, Board of Estimate and other city officials, as soon as possible, with respect to a possible solution. There was to be no staff, no money, no specific instructions and no prior commitments. I was totally free to do as I saw fit and to report precisely what I felt.

Deputy Mayor Ed Hamilton came in. He talked for a few minutes. The media had made him out to be an automaton type—a kind of fleshy IBM machine. He's that, all right, but I suspect a good deal more. Although he may not have Aurelio's easy openness, he's clearly brilliant and he would certainly help here. No meaningful discussion of Forest Hills can be conducted without involvement in the fiscal aspects and that's Hamilton's forte. Jay Kriegel, Nat Leventhal and Marvin Schick came in. Why Schick, the mayor's liaison with the city's Jewish groups? Is it really the "Jewish community" that's involved, and even if it is, is it wise to focus on that? More offers to help—"Just ask, Mario. Anything you need!"

But what? There's hardly been time to think about it and outside there are a dozen newsmen and five television cameras waiting. I had some reluctance about facing them. No one who goes to court likes being in the pit without preparation; every question should be anticipated, every answer prepackaged. "Maybe we should put this off until tomorrow—let's think about it." "No, that won't do. They expect to hear something today and if they don't get it from you they'll make it up. Give it your best shot." Since there was no time to prepare, there was nothing to do but answer the questions simply.

It seemed to go fairly well.

Simeon Golar had come into the mayor's office midway through our meeting. It wasn't difficult to read his displeasure and it was understandable. He had been out front on this issue for months taking the flack for his hard stand. He himself suggested accommodation and compromise of sorts but had been told to stand fast. It wasn't easy for him now to step aside while someone else—an outsider—came in to "set things right." I made no attempt at softening him; I'm not very good at that anyway. I made a simple request for cooperation and he, just as simply and coolly, agreed to give it.

I wonder if he thinks that the mayor has arranged something with me that hasn't been disclosed? I know many people probably do—or at least I've been told that already. But why? Don't they know about my history of disagreement with the mayor? Probably, the Corona situation has created the impression that we have always worked hand in glove with the mayor. Vito Battista and Assemblyman Herb Miller did their best to create the belief that the Corona compromise was a rigged deal to get Lindsay off the hook and apparently they've had some success. It's annoying how easy it is to play the "big lie" game. Just a little plausibility, a very big mouth, and a hungry group of media people are all that's needed.

Golar stood all through my television interviews—I could "feel" him behind me, listening intently. He's wrong about this or at least my part in it, but that will have to be proven to him.

Many of the preliminary decisions were actually made as a result of the questions put by the media people. One of these was the timetable. They wanted to know how soon we would report. After some quick calculating, taking into account particularly the fact that the project was already well into construction, we said we'd try to get it done within six weeks.

Friday, May 19, 1972

They've jumped all over my six-week target date. Hal Levenson of Channel 13 said it can't be done. But what choice do we have? Since the mayor won't stop the construction, time *is* of the essence. On the other hand, the time I've allowed myself may be unrealistically short—all we can do is try.

Levenson, who is probably among the most knowledgeable

people in the city on Forest Hills, having studied and reported upon it a number of times during the past year, also told me I was nuts to have accepted the assignment. He feels nothing I can do will resolve the problem and that it will be damaging to me personally. "Well!"

It is already apparent that this assignment will place a very great strain on the firm. I was in court this morning trying to protect the Long Island College Hospital against the community assault on our Hoagland Lab Plan.* It wasn't easy to take the "establishment" role and the case is going to need a great deal of work. Added to the fact that my secretary's gone and one of our attorneys has decided to "retire" to a civil service job, it makes for a considerable headache.

At least I'm managing to get a deal done on the phone without leaving the office. The calls are coming in at a frantic pace and it's already clear that the opponents of the project are well organized. While publicly indicating a pique at the mayor for having named me without their approval and a reluctance to deal with me, they nevertheless have called in great numbers to establish the connection. I'm keeping a careful list because I will eventually have to sit down with all of them.

The other side of the issue has been strongly silent. The quick impression is that there may be no strong feeling in the black community for the project, but that's probably not the fact. One of the difficulties is that the black side of the question is hard to identify. On the Forest Hills side, geography is enough to isolate and mark the adversary—we know who and where they are and that makes communication relatively easy. But unless the Housing Authority is regarded as the other party in interest, it's difficult to say who is. Dealing with the H.A. is, of course, mechanically easy. Presumably, however, the H.A. represents a point of view that is

---

* The Long Island College Hospital is located in downtown Brooklyn. The Hoagland Laboratory property, which was part of the hospital complex, had been partially destroyed by fire. The hospital wished to demolish it; the community, concerned about what might replace it, was opposed. Litigation ensued and the writer, whose firm was general counsel to the hospital, appeared on behalf of the hospital.

shared by the low income community that would benefit from the development. If that's the fact, it would be good to deal beyond the H.A. with that community itself. I'll have to talk with Golar about this if things don't change after Sunday's *Newsmakers* show. That exposure might turn things around.

Jerry Birbach has called again. He's actually a reasonable fellow and, in a lot of ways, likable. Apparently he feels driven to his posturing by his political ambitions. I think he's hurt his cause by announcing for office (against State Senator Emanuel Gold) and I have the feeling he knows that too. He also seems to feel that dealing publicly with me would make him vulnerable because his only hope for success depends upon his maintaining a high-pitched, emotional issue as his standard.

In the course of our discussion he said a number of things that I might ordinarily have argued with him about. I didn't. I'll have to resist the temptation to be an advocate so long as I'm in this role. It's much easier being an advocate. The restraint and patience required of the middleman in our situation are hard virtues to cultivate. I'm particularly concerned about my ability to do it on Sunday. The CBS show will be the first—and probably the last—opportunity to establish some credibility on a broad scale and to do that I'll have to remain objective.

Saturday, May 20, 1972

I was able to catch up on the week's work for the firm and take the daily ration of twenty or so F.H. calls today. The calls are clogging the firm's switchboard and fouling my work schedule but I'll have to keep taking them. The important thing is to hear from as many of the people interested as possible. So far the sentiments expressed are almost uniformly encouraging. Even Birbach's attitude is a good one; he's been careful not to attack me personally.

I spoke with Vinny Albanese this evening after a conversation with Jim Breslin on the phone. Breslin, as usual, emits ideas like sparks from a Chinese wheel—every once in a while one catches fire. He's strong on the possibility of including a preference for Vietnamese veterans in any project. I can see some merit in the suggestion but my lawyer's caution tells me to ease off the idea for the time being. It has some crude implications on the security issue. Moreover, I don't think the time is yet ripe for getting too deeply into specifics. This first stage must be devoted to a study of the facts. The argument has been conducted so far with very little attention being given to the hard legal and physical realities, and the job of getting the facts down is going to be one of the most difficult challenges here, given the time problem. But it's indispensable. We must know everything about the history of this project, its relationship to Corona, how it was chosen, why, the nature of the site, the construction contracts, the constitutional law, the agency regulations and much more, even before we attempt meaningful discussions. There's no other intelligent way. But it won't be easy. I understand Dr. Newman at N.Y.U. has spent hundreds of thousands of dollars and a few years studying this problem and still is not ready to reach conclusions.

Vinny Albanese, being the fine lawyer he is, appreciates this and is accordingly easy to talk to. He made some good suggestions about tomorrow's show, but even Vin, whom I know fairly well and who, presumably, knows me just as well, asked the inevitable question, "Why did you agree to do this?" The common impression seems to be that there is no chance of personal gain to the man in the middle and, therefore, there is no good reason for assuming that posture. Are things really that bad? Is it naïve to believe that someone just might want to do this thing because it's a right thing to do? Or are they right and am I kidding myself. That may deserve some thought when we're through, but there's no time to worry about it now.

Sunday, May 21, 1972

The show was the thing. I left the studio feeling I had blown it. There were a dozen things I wanted to say and didn't and a couple of things I didn't say well. It was like the feeling you get when you walk out of court. On the way home WINS carried the Vietnam Vet bit and someone else mentioned my disagreement with Golar as to the "bigots." I had answered that question as tightly as possible. I didn't say there weren't bigots; I said I wouldn't make that moral judgment. Not a particularly fine distinction but one which apparently escaped or was ignored by the reporters.

All afternoon and into the evening the calls came. The show went over much better than I expected it would. Apparently some credibility and acceptance have been established.

My statement that I would not regard Birbach's reluctance to participate in any discussions as a problem, since there were other responsible voices like Assemblyman Jack Gallagher and Senator Martin Knorr on his side of the issue, reached him. He called tonight to say he would like to talk to me, but not until after the primary. He doesn't want to show his people any "weakness." He was pleasant.

More study today—it's tough stuff. I'm reading everything I can get my hands on, as fast as possible. There's an awful lot there.

Monday, May 22, 1972

The Association of the Bar of the City of New York Judiciary Committee meeting on the Court of Appeals candidates* took most of the day, but I was able to take several calls.

I spent the night in F.H. again, anonymously, and spoke with several people all utterly opposed to *any* project. It's extraordinary how poorly informed they actually are; that's clearly one of the major problems. They have numerous erroneous versions of the critical facts and it's kind of late in the day to start disabusing them of their wrong notions.

Al Lashinsky of the Queens Jewish Community Council called tonight to say that he would have a press conference tomorrow with several other Jewish leaders whom he claims represent, cumulatively, three hundred thousand Jews! Who can dispute it? But who can prove it? He was guarded in talking to me—his distrust of almost everybody involved in the situation is obvious. His only real reason for calling me was to size me up. It'll take a while, but I think we'll be able to reach him eventually.

---

* The Judiciary Committee regularly reports on the qualifications of candidates for judicial office. The writer was a member of the Committee at the time.

Tuesday, May 23, 1972

Lashinsky's press conference was nothing more than an attempt to establish an identification for his group. It was also an opportunity for them to relieve themselves of their pique with Lindsay for not talking to them, particularly, before appointing me. I told Lashinsky on the phone last night and again tonight that I regarded this as little more than game-playing. I still anticipate no real difficulty in talking with him or his people.

More study tonight.

Wednesday, May 24, 1972

Jay Kriegel, the mayor's brainy assistant, was on the phone today to tell me his man Warren had pulled together some background material for me to read; I should have them tomorrow.

Most of the day was spent analyzing the *Gautreaux* case in Chicago and the law surrounding it. That's apparently the last word on the constitutional requirement to provide scatter-site housing. In effect, the court there has held that unless cities use a respectable portion of their federal housing subsidy to move low-income blacks into white areas, they may forfeit their entire allotment of funds. Obviously, that would be disastrous in this city.

Like *Brown v. The Board of Education*, the genesis of these rulings, the *Gautreaux* doctrine is judicially responsive but probably out of touch with the public consensus. This often happens in a nation ruled by laws and not outcry.

Thursday, May 25, 1972

I talked to Golar today and told him about the failure of communication from the black groups. He's still quite reticent and circumspect with me and I can't blame him. He explained that leaders like Ken Clark and Roy Wilkins would not agree to call me; I would have to call them. I've always been impatient with this kind of protocol but I may do it. Golar promised to have other interested groups who favor the project call me to open lines of communication.

I was in F.H. again tonight—more of the same except there is now some reason to believe that there are a substantial number of people who favor the project but are reluctant to say so publicly.

I met a few people who recognized me tonight—even unshaven and in sport shirt—so I'll not be able to make any informal samplings for much longer. I think I got better answers before I was recognized.

I was at the site this morning and spoke to the men in the shed. It's clear the pilings won't be complete until late summer at the earliest. I met some protesters at the site and had my first "confrontation." Aside from some Battista-inspired jabs about Corona, it went fairly well.

Friday, May 26, 1972

The Long Island College Hospital case was on again this morning. It took the entire morning and a lot of my energy; I was beat after it.

The calls from the "Jewish community" continue, but now there's a mixture; many of them favor the project as is. But most of these people are not residents and those that are will not speak for publication.

This weekend must be spent in hard study. My affidavit was filed in *Lefrak*; I'll do L.I.C.H. tomorrow A.M. and the rest of the weekend will be free for the real tedium.

Saturday, May 27, 1972

I took a few minutes this morning to look back on the past ten days and to assess the situation at this point. The original plan of approach (such as it was) was to be phased as follows: factual study; gathering community sentiment; constructing a plan (if any could be constructed); report to the mayor. What hadn't been taken into account was the necessity for establishing an identity for the "middleman." That has taken more time than I expected it would. The publicity has been extensive in all the media on an almost daily basis. Today there was a "Man in the News" story in the *Post*. It was carefully done by Andy Soltis, although he *did* make my parents Sicilians and had me "commuting" Walter Scher's sentence. It was entirely too personal, however. Beside being embarrassing, I think that kind of "personal" exposure is not good for the role I'm supposed to fill. I would much prefer to come off as vague in personal detail—generally objective and honest, but nondimensional beyond that.

Looking back, it's clear that the community sentiment is strongly for resolution. I've received dozens of offers of help, including a number from former students of mine at St. John's law school. It's encouraging.

Today I received two lists of names from Golar's office with a strong suggestion that I call them, notwithstanding his telling me yesterday he would have them contact me. I'm afraid its more game-playing—this time from the other side—and I don't want to play. While I'd like to speak to as many interested people as I can, I think it would be a mistake to reach out for some at the risk of ignoring others. I'll stay with my announced idea of talking to anyone who contacts me.

I met with Breslin tonight on my way into Forest Hills. He was deeply into McGovern strategy and we talked about that for a while. I still think that McGovern's tax issue comes off so pat and simple that it will be regarded as flimflammery. Certainly most people will not have the time or the ability to analyze the issue and will deal with superficial aspects of it. On the surface, it looks too easy and is vulnerable to surface criticism.

McGovern's "boggles the mind" phraseology has to go. I said to J.B. that it would be nice for once to have a candidate who never uses cliché—that alone might get him elected! I also thought that McGovern's reaching to mention his "bomber-pilot" days was demeaning and unnecessary.

Withal he's still riding high. But he's really still in the gym as far as the big fight is concerned.

We couldn't let all this McGovern talk go on without getting into F.H. Breslin asked whether McGovern could be helpful some way.

I told him I'd think about it. But it seems to me—no politician will want to get into this situation if he can avoid it.

A couple of hours of reading before sleep—but at times I could barely see the pages. I've already read hundreds of pages of sociological studies, dozens of cases and at least a score of position papers. The Court of Appeals experience and fifteen years of "quick reading and education" have certainly helped. Thinking about it now, I believe it would not have been useful to have a staff even if one could have been supplied. The relay time to get the information from the staff to me would have been a problem. Then too, there's nothing like doing your own research for developing a command.

I'm beginning to realize too how helpful the experience of the last twelve years has been. I hadn't ever thought about it before, but much of that time was spent learning things that are now invaluable to me. I've been involved with housing and the scatter-site program since Sheepshead Bay in 1967. The work with Community Boards and all the administrative city law I've learned—the numerous lawsuits against the city on behalf of various community groups—are paying off.

Sunday, May 28, 1972

Assemblyman Miller was heard from today. A release in this morning's *Times* had him suggesting that the governor consider reopening the question of a swap of sites with Corona. They're back again! That's been a troublesome suggestion for the last year. Of course, a couple of years ago the idea of moving the high school to 108th Street was first in the order of logic. I pushed the argument very hard on Aurelio at the meeting Breslin arranged and which eventually produced a solution. But he was told by Golar that the project at 108th Street was viable and should not be touched. It was only when I became convinced of that commitment that my Corona compromise was suggested.

At that time there were also some mutterings about returning the low-income housing site to Lewis Avenue in Corona and using

108th for the school. That suggestion too had a sort of geometrical appeal to it—but it wasn't practical.

So much has happened in two years—the compromise is nearly a *fait accompli* to the delight of hundreds of thousands of parents in Forest Hills–Rego Park–Kew Gardens; design work on the school and surveying are complete; they can start clearing almost immediately. To move this site now would mean a waste of the millions that have already been spent. But worse than that, from the city's point of view, it would mean commencing the cumbersome site-selection process all over again. If they did, it could be stymied—just as it was by us—for another four or five years.

And in the end, what would become of scatter-site housing? It's one thing to reject this project's dimensions; it's quite another to kill it completely. One is consistent with the concept; the other rejects the concept's workability entirely. At least, that is the common apprehension of the situation, and here—as elsewhere in government and politics—the common apprehension is probably more relevant than the truth.

Birbach and Emanuel Gold debated on Channel 4 today at 2:30. Gold was smooth, sincere, intelligent. Birbach was jowly, gruff, unprepared—but effective! Jerry has a flair for banging away at simple superficial issues with blunt slogans, undeterred by what is actually the subject of discussion. He was almost cruel in his repeated dropping of poor Sy Thaler's name in an attempt to associate Gold with Sy.* But he is obviously responsive to a growing militancy in this town's middle class.

And while Jerry is making the voice of "his" community clear, I continue to have difficulty finding a "black" voice. I went to Cunningham Park early this morning knowing that a lot of the blacks from South Jamaica would be there in family groups. I took a few shots with some of the fathers and sons on the basketball court and eventually struck up a good conversation. These blacks were fortunate enough to have houses of their own in Hollis, Queens. They unhesitatingly said that they would not want the

---

* Seymour Thaler, former state senator from Queens County and elected justice of the Supreme Court was indicted and eventually convicted in 1972.

project in *their* neighborhood. They feel that many of the whites who oppose in Forest Hills are bigots, but then in an interesting contradiction they themselves admit they would oppose it in their own neighborhoods.

It becomes clearer and clearer that this project is measured by most people in terms of its immediate effect on them and their property. No one but the "idealists"—who are sufficiently remote from the problem so that they are not really challenged by it—seem to favor it as it's now planned. But even if that were true, would it—should it—be determinative? Mightn't it be right to recognize that selfishness and to reach beyond it? Or is Birbach right? Is the community—right or wrong—to have its way? Consider what that would mean. I suspect that here, as in most of these situations, the truth lies somewhere in the middle.

Monday, May 29, 1972

On Channel 4 tonight they used a portion of the film taken earlier this week at the site. Hopefully, that will end the publicity until we have something to report. It will be a great saving of time if we're able to avoid the media for the time being, although they have been helpful and fair—so far.

Tuesday, May 30, 1972

Gold called this morning and said he was having difficulty reaching Borough President Manes about getting space in the Borough Hall building, so I called Manes myself. It's important to have a meeting place somewhere in Queens, and Borough Hall makes a good deal of practical sense. His first concern was the effect the office might have on the appearance of objectivity. He was also concerned about the possibility of pickets congregating at the building. I told him that should be no problem in view of the fact that I would take appointments only, and the community understood that. He said he would talk to his P.R. man, Marvin Cohen, about it and get back to me. Gold called later to say he'd spoken to Manes, and it "looked good." If I don't hear by Thursday I'll make my own arrangements.

Owen Moritz of the *Daily News* called looking for a story but was quickly discouraged. He wanted to go out on one of the "walking tours" but I told him the publicity had cost me my anonymity, so that my nocturnal visits couldn't serve the same purpose they had for the last couple of weeks. He's extremely well informed and offered some helpful background information. Moritz is grim on the prospects for a compromise. His feeling is that there are definite "racist" feelings which will not be put off by anything less than a total avoidance of the project. He's certain that whatever report I make will have everyone unhappy and me despised. He said it would definitely hurt my "political" prospects.

Marty Gallent called again. He was helpful. As a former Community Board chairman in the affected area and a City Planning commissioner since then, he has a good background both in knowledgeability and expertise. Marty mentioned the "236" * compromise about which I've heard from a number of sources— apparently it began with Gallent. He's also going to send me his "spray" scatter-site paper. Essentially, what he's recommending is that the project's composition be altered so as to include a good number of middle-income tenants through the use of various subsidies like 236 and that such mixed units be proliferated in other

---

* Section 236 of the National Housing Act assists lower-income families in obtaining rental or cooperative housing by providing the sponsor of a newly constructed, rehabilitated or existing project with payments to the bank or other approved private lender to reduce the purchaser's mortgage payments to a sum equaling a debt service charge at 1 percent interest. This program may also be used to subsidize a non-FHA-insured mortgage for a project receiving state or local government interest, as in a Mitchell-Lama project. Eligibility for payment to a project availing itself of Section 236 benefits is generally limited to families whose adjusted incomes do not exceed 135 percent of the maximum income prescribed for initial admission to New York City federally aided public-housing projects. Effectively, this describes a group whose income is 35 percent higher than that of the group which is commonly referred to as "low-income."

In the confusing jargon of the housing mystique, the Section 236 group is sometimes referred to as the "lower-income" segment as distinguished from the "low-income" segment.

areas of Queens. He would assign a specific number of units to a particular planning district and then let the locality work out the details.

In the course of the discussion I mentioned to Marty the possibility that other scatter-site planning in the county ought to await the experience at Forest Hills should a project be built. He thought that would make sense.

Marty agreed that no one speaks effectively for the low-income segment of our town. I pointed out that I had heard from very few blacks or anyone else who would state, let along articulate in detail, any case for the project. He said the City Planning Commission had regularly been disappointed at the failure of any substantial showing by the low-income community. It still looks like Golar is the only available party "for."

But is this surprising? If the low-income stratum had a real voice, would it *be* low-income? Why should it surprise anyone that this group—for the most part uneducated and socially disadvantaged—should be without organization and self-constructed vehicles of expression? Isn't it especially this group that should have the right to expect the elected and appointed official to serve as its voice? After all, it wasn't until the last decade that even our middle-income—and higher—groups found the ability and willingness to organize effectively and speak out as they have in Forest Hills, Forest Hills Gardens and Sagamore Douglaston. Wasn't Corona without a voice until the courts gave them impact, Vito Battista used them as a battleground and Breslin got involved?

Seymour Samuels of the Queens Jewish Community Council called for reassurance that I would be available to his group. I explained to him I was still trying to get into the facts sufficiently to be able to speak knowledgeably with him. We chatted until I had to hang up to catch McGovern–Humphrey in their second debate. He seemed content.

I've been through all the lawsuits and found a mine of information. It becomes increasingly difficult to absorb all that I need to know in a hurry while still trying to keep an oar in at the office. Tomorrow will be two weeks and I haven't even begun thinking positively about solutions.

Wednesday, May 31, 1972

I've decided to try to get some special research help. Mickey Beller of the mayor's legislative office was in to see me at 32 Court Street, 7:30 this A.M. He had to get a 9:30 plane to Albany but we were able to get in an hour's conversation. I tried to describe the genesis of the mayor's idea and what has occurred in the last two weeks. I explained that in my view the heart of the opposition is the fact of crime and "decay" and that I regarded the argument as both sincere and understandable. I suggested that this be his first area of research: What has been the experience with other projects? How does the experience vary with locale and physical composition of the project? What can be done to contain or mitigate the problem? He'll get to work on it tomorrow.

In passing, I pointed out that the large size of the existent F.H. community and its stability should make it easier to cope with irritants or threats from a low-income project. One of the things we'll have to study is whether there has ever been a scatter-site project in an area as strong as Forest Hills.

Mickey is bright, well-educated, and willing. He, like everyone else apparently, regards the likelihood of achieving anything as very slim. I'm all the more impressed with his willingness to try in view of that appraisal.

Joe Goldstein called from Nassau County to say that he had no interest in Forest Hills other than my involvement. He suggested that all multiple bedroom apartments be eliminated. He was sure this would please the opponents. So am I, but the problem is obviously not susceptible to that kind of simplistic solution. If the project is justifiable at all, it is because of what it does for the low-income group *most in need*. But wouldn't that be the families? Shouldn't the emphasis be on lifting the children out of their environment and providing them with a better opportunity for fulfillment? In fact, the more one attempts to justify the project as it now is the more difficult it becomes, not because it doesn't serve a need but perhaps because it does not serve the need well enough.

But then, is it really for me to say whether the project is good or bad as an absolute? I'm to find "facts" and display them. I'd rather do more. It's difficult trying to suspend individual judgment—it's easier to make the ultimate decision than to merely "state." I'm more and more convinced I'd rather argue than arbitrate.

Helen Lazar of the Forest Hills Neighbors group called and said she was afraid I was talking to the wrong people. She was reassured before I hung up. Assemblyman Joe Lisa called and was eager to help. He said he had some ideas about transportation; I told him I'd be in touch with him. Joe tells me Herb Miller is ripping me all over town, saying that I polarized Queens' Italian heart—Corona. I've never understood exactly what set Herb off against me. I can recall vividly the days before the compromise when Herb and I were cordial.

I suspect that Battista—who has an amazing ability to paralyze the intellects of brighter people, maybe with decibels—has somehow mesmerized Herb as well. I'm not sure it's worth worrying about, except that Herb is an effective voice in Forest Hills.

Thursday, June 1, 1972

Tempus fugit.

Why not Sam Lefrak? Given a willingness on his part to speak to me, I think it would be worthwhile trying it. Perhaps the next meeting of the Chemical Advisory Board would be a good opportunity. He should have some ideas on the mix possibilities.

This morning I thought I had something, but it went up in smoke this afternoon. The Board of Estimate decision in 1966 specifically referred to the proposed use of Saultell Ave.—a small street on the southeast corner of the project area. That would have required a map change and the decision specifically noted that one should be sought. They haven't had one. Of course, if one were necessary now it would put this matter back into the City Planning Commission and Board of Estimate just as Corona and Lindenwood were. Later in the day Irwin Fruchtman from City Planning told me the street wasn't necessary and that's why they had no map change. I'll check it out for myself, but I don't think there's much to it.

Peter Ferguson, of Operation Open City called—with a chip on his shoulder at the outset. He wanted to know if I would come to them for a meeting and I explained it would be easier if his group came out to Queens. He agreed. I told him I was doing this with everybody.

I tried discussing the merits with Ferguson, but he wouldn't get too deep into the subject. Like so many others involved, he keeps his dialogue at a superficial level. I asked him casually about cutting down on the size of the buildings or converting one of the two buildings into a mixed unit. He was opposed to any change. On the matter of crime he felt the answer was more police and strict enforcement by the Housing Authority. Not exactly a subtle solution. I told Ferguson I'd get back to him.

I talked with Aurelio today. He's on his way to Rome for a week and just called to ask whether he could be helpful. It's always good to talk with him. I remain convinced that he is one of the few professional politicians whose innate integrity overcomes the strong pragmatic drive. He's believable and sensitive. His only suggestion today was to postpone anything meaningful until after the primaries so as to avoid as far as possible the political connotations.

I spoke with Rabbi Grunblatt of Forest Hills. Talking at this stage is still a matter of generalization because I'm not yet sufficiently in command of the facts to be able to deal with particular proposals.

My mentor Professor Rose Trapani called today and said I was foolish for getting involved because nothing good could come of it. She's thinking in terms of total solutions leaving everyone content, and I will, of course, concede that's impossible. But can't we be helpful in at least defusing the situation? There must be some intermediate plan that will give something to everyone; that will at least reduce the roar to a grumble. Of course, if there were some way to reach the best moral and spiritual instincts of all concerned, the problem would be simple. That's where the total answer lies to everything. All the philosophers, through all the ages, have said precisely the same thing: The single best rule for the intelligent conduct of life and society is "love." The perfect answer. Unfortunately, however, that is plainly too much to ask. They still put people on crosses for that kind of thing.

Rose said that if I suggested a compromise and it was implemented I would be accused by the "No Project" people of having been responsible for low-income in their community and by the blacks for having deprived them of units; no one would remember that I was starting with three 24-story towers and not from scratch.

I think Rose is wrong; I have more respect for the intelligence and fairness of the people involved. But even if she's right, what difference will it make if in fact the compromise resolves the present impasse?

Friday, June 2, 1972

By day's end I had put myself two weeks ahead of the game in the Pacific Street Block Association–Long Island College Hospital case, had assigned most of my other current work and prepared to dispose of the rest tomorrow. This will leave me relatively free for following up on various leads in F.H. I'll have to stay around the office—particularly with the hiring of two new lawyers and the changes being made—but I'll have no absorbing firm work for a while.

I spoke with the Ethical Culture Society of Queens, Joe Mattone, Dan Bayer of the Housing Development Administration, Ed Lee of the Housing Authority, and Senator Gold today. Nothing exciting was produced. Lee convinced me that a map change was not needed and Gold said Manes was going to offer me an office in Borough Hall in a release late this afternoon. Gold is taking no part in the arrangements. His overriding concern for the moment is his primary with Birbach and he's maintaining a strict objectivity where I'm involved. He said he would and his word is really gold.

There are, it seems to me, two key factors yet to be resolved and whose resolution may determine the course of this entire process. One is the lawsuit to be argued in the Court of Appeals in Albany next week. If the residents were to win, the entire matter would be returned to the Board of Estimate where the borough presidents,

Beame and Garelik, would have to decide how to disengage themselves. If the residents lose, what bargaining weapon do they have left? Given an exhaustion of remedies, in the legislature and courts, their only remaining weapons would be the threat of violence or exodus. If a residents' defeat in the Court of Appeals is coupled with a Birbach defeat in the primary, it may soften their position somewhat. While I can take no active part in either the lawsuit or the election I have to make myself knowledgeable on both. I'm guessing the residents will lose in court and Birbach in the primary. I think most observers agree Gold should win overall; the more pertinent test is whether he will win in Forest Hills proper. The majority sentiment is Birbach will win big in Forest Hills but will lose overall.

Saturday, June 3, 1972

I read the Congressional Record for a good part of the afternoon tracing back the legislative history of the 1949 Housing Act. Actually it's not terribly helpful. Mostly, the intention as described in the reports was painted in broad strokes: the need for housing generally, the particular plight of the low-income, the need for federal subsidy—all now accepted general propositions. The hard part is the application of those good principles to this specific situation and that will call for, as the next step, a study of the scatter-site refinement of the principle. That's what Warren was supposed to have for me but hasn't produced. If the energy he's manifested is any indication there won't be a great deal of assistance coming from his office.

Dave Minkin, the builder, and I talked for a few minutes in Brooklyn. He thinks the idea of a mix of middle-income with low is a good one, but not if it's limited to one of the three towers. His judgment as a builder is good and he feels the 236 would not be attractive on the same site with the pure low-income.

The owners of properties on Atlantic Avenue in Brooklyn scheduled for condemnation in connection with the Schermerhorn Urban Renewal Project were in this afternoon. It's the same old story. The condemnation of their property will be a mistake; their politicians deserted them; they can't relocate. Why did the city save similar properties and decide to take *them?* What can they do now? Why won't the courts help them?

All the same questions; all the old answers. I'll decide next week whether to bring a suit. If we do, it'll be the beginning of another drawn out "war" with the city. It would be quite a thing if, while working as the city's fact-finder in Forest Hills, I were to be simultaneously fighting them on Atlantic Avenue. I checked it out with Ed Hamilton and he agreed that my assignment was a "no strings" arrangement and that I was free to proceed as usual. But prudence may require something else.

Sunday, June 4, 1972

I've heard from none of the people who were going to do research for me. Apparently, I'll have to do without that help.

Some "friend" is saving all the clippings containing negative and derogatory comments about my role; I found a few more in an anonymous letter that had been in Saturday's mail but wasn't opened until today. Somebody's getting his kicks out of this anyway.

Monday, June 5, 1972

Seymour Samuels called again, this time to say that his group was concerned over how I would read the results of the Birbach–Gold primary. His worry was that a Gold victory might be interpreted as a vote "for" the project. He indicated his group did not favor Birbach but would be forced to come out for him if there were any chance the project would be encouraged by a Gold victory. I explained to Seymour that personally I had no respect for a political judgment that would make the vote turn on the single issue of compromise or no compromise. I also pointed out to him that I did not think the result would mean much practically because in the end the only judgment that would mean anything would be the judgment for or against whatever proposals we might make.

I have reduced our analysis down to a few or perhaps several hard-core areas of investigation that need study. Unfortunately, neither Warren nor Beller have gotten back to me, so that I'll have to pick up the matters I asked them to help with.

I spent tonight with Marino Jeantet in Queens. Marino tells me his Community Board is strongly against the project and would probably be unhappy with anything like the project as it now is. His judgment is an important one. There are few people in Queens who know more about civic affairs or who are more to be trusted.

Tuesday, June 6, 1972

I met with Manes this morning. He's been cooperative. The conference room will be available to me Monday through Thursday from six on.

Mrs. Stein,* a resident, called me at the office, and after expressing her "shock" at being able to get me "personally" she said she was against the project. She was confused about the "facts": she thought the piling would cost four million dollars; that Lefrak owned the site and lost millions of dollars in a futile effort to build foundations. She also believed that a number of buildings had sunk at the site and were now part of the subsoil. "At least, the buildings should be cut in half even if it costs the city fifteen million dollars." Asked how other taxpayers might feel about giving up fifteen million dollars to assuage the fears of the F.H. people, she said she didn't care. This woman will be extremely difficult to please.

Mayor Lindsay called just to find out if he could be helpful. I brought him up to date. We agreed there was no point in meeting for the time being.

Pete McLoughlin of the *Daily News* was on the phone after receiving Manes' release. I told him flatly that if Birbach is saying I refuse to deal with him he's not telling the truth and I would have no objection to his saying so in an article. While I'm prepared to be diplomatic, I don't think it will serve any good purpose to permit

* A pseudonym.

anyone to befog the issue with misstatements, particularly where they may have the effect of weakening the report's credibility.

Two more problems have arisen; they could compound the confusion here. The first is the failure of the governor to sign the Corona bill embodying the compromise. Unless he does so by Thursday, there will be a new chapter opened in the Corona battle. In effect, it will put us back to where we were three years ago. I would have to reenter that fight actively. The single most apparent argument then would be to move the school to 108th Street and my position at that point could become untenable. We'll know in forty-eight hours.

The other problem is presented by the Harbor Village situation in Brooklyn. Harbor Village is a Mitchell-Lama that received Board of Estimate approval some time ago. There is a chance it will be reconsidered and killed by the Board of Estimate tomorrow, despite the fact that contracts have been let. The UAW, the sponsor of the project, as well as the contractor, are furious. The mayor is apparently upset over it but he's not able to get anyone with him. The implications for Forest Hills are clear: if Harbor Village, then why not F.H.? Although I believe there's a legal difference between the two situations I'm not sure the public at large would understand or accept it.

If F.H were to be returned to the Board at this point the matter would quite clearly no longer require an independent agent. It would then be a purely political matter again. The possibilities are serious. A killing of Harbor Village and/or F.H. in this fashion would carry with it lawsuits, a crisis of confidence in the stability of city enactments by the board, gross confusion, and a general disrespect for governmental operation. But the community sentiment is powerful and their arguments are not without substance.

Wednesday, June 7, 1972

A busy and productive day.

Miss Ethel Halman,* a spinster who lives with her mother in

* A pseudonym.

Forest Hills, called to talk about her opposition to the project. Her position was consistent with the others I've heard; its almost as though they were speaking from a prepared text. The theme generally is that the low-income project results in decay and eventual destruction of the surrounding middle-class community. The evidence for this is usually quite meager. Typically, when pressed, the best Miss Halman could do was to point to St. Louis and to Crown Heights. The suggestion that there might be a distinction between F.H. and other areas not quite so firmly established is ignored. But the conviction is undiminished by the failure of specific proof; I'm inclined to think that no matter what statistics and evidence we're able to marshal, this community's fear will not be totally dissipated. One story of a mugging at a project—whether or not true—will overcome in their minds any array of statistics. The syllogism is simple: Welfare and Blacks are generally responsible for a great deal of crime; there are Welfare and Blacks in projects; there will be a great deal of crime in and around the project.

And then, too, there is a quick projection from the problem of crime—however real, fancied, or exaggerated—to all other middle-class complaints: taxes, education, etc. All of these may be legitimate, but this coupling of them with the crime problem results eventually in an indictment of the project for all the sins against the middle class.

This fear is so ingrained that even if unjustified (and I don't believe it can fairly be said that it is totally unjustified) it must be assuaged somehow. If that can't be done by intellectualizing, then perhaps it should be done by eliminating the source of the fear as much as possible. Is that a "compromise" with principle? Not necessarily. The principle is the validity of serving the need of the low-income segment of our community. But that need is perhaps better served by a project that is acceptable to the community and assured of its cooperation. Then, too, the elimination of some low-income and welfare could be accompanied by the satisfying of other obvious needs. The problem of the elderly is certainly one, as is society's debt to the Vietnam veteran. And back to the middle class—isn't housing for them a good, particularly if its low-middle class, say $10–12,000 per annum?

Why not one tower for Mitchell-Lama* middle-income assisted by 236 subsidies?

1. There is a need for middle-income units.

2. It will provide a certain amount of economic integration internal to the complex itself.

3. It will have private sponsorship and the advantages that the sponsor's selfish instincts will produce, such as keeping his project safe and attractive.

4. It can be sold without undoing the construction contract or returning to the Board of Estimate. (Consider the practical and political problems this would avoid, particularly in light of Harbor Village.)

5. It would avoid the tragedy of expending large sums of money to reduce the buildings.

6. It will reduce substantially the number of units for low-income, including welfare.

Now add to it:

Forty percent of the units for the elderly as originally proposed. These elderly are low-income and who can argue about their need? They could be either in one residence or sprinkled through the other two towers, and this would leave 224 units of low-income in the third building. This number could be pushed back to 280 for a full third of the overall project, reducing the elderly to one third. Of this only a percentage (to be obtained) would be welfare. Say 10 percent—which would mean about 28 of the original 840 units, or a little over three percent would be welfare. Surely, the low-income community will object that they have given up too much. But in fact, 280 units is clearly more in keeping with the original intendment of scatter-site and there may be other places in Queens or Manhattan where the loss can be recaptured.

* "Mitchell-Lama" is the popular name for the New York State Limited Private Housing Companies law which permits city and state loans and assistance in the form of tax abatement to private rental and cooperative housing for lower- and middle-income families. The New York City Board of Estimate must approve costs and rents.

We tried this on Commissioner Walter Fried of the Housing Authority today. He seemed to like it and said it was similar to something the H.A. had earlier suggested. He sees a problem in getting federal 236 funds, but we can work on that. Golar was not so sanguine; even at a mere suggestion of it he made his case for the necessity of avoiding *any* loss of low-income units. This will require compensating.

Sam Briedner, a civic leader from Queens, also had some comments. He points out, and I think accurately, that any representations as to mix will be rejected by the community unless there is an "iron-clad" assurance that it will be legally enforceable. We should consider the possibility of a contract with a Mitchell-Lama sponsor specifically referring to the composition of the other two towers. Briedner says the idea of cooperatives is appealing. I haven't yet looked into it thoroughly but have started to. It presents problems. Although conceptually attractive, the legal parts don't fit neatly.

Thursday, June 8, 1972

On the chance that the 236 idea is a good one, I called Fred Perrotta today and asked about how to get federal help. He suggested that the necessary starting point would have to be S. William Green of the Department of Housing and Urban Development. Fred agreed to help if our idea passed muster with Green. I'll have to get to him. Perrotta is honest and capable and can be a big help here, particularly since he's well connected with both Rockefeller and Nixon.

It's just impossible to shut out all the many other obligations that need attending to and this is making it extremely difficult to do the kind of concentrated work this thing needs. Corona is now down to the wire. How cruel to let the guillotine swing so close—we only have until midnight before the thirty-day period for the governor to sign the compromise bill expires. The homeowners have been praying for the last three weeks. I expect the bill to be signed, and anticipating that, I've written a kind of "wrap-up" letter to the community. We'll know by tomorrow afternoon.

And the maneuvering goes on! Apparently, a group from Queens (I'm guessing its Samuels' group) went to Manes last week and pressed for a reconsideration of the matter at the Board of Estimate. Although this group has spoken to me several times, they never mentioned it, nor did Manes during our discussion earlier this week. Actually, Manes is now on the spot, particularly in view of Harbor Village. If he votes for reconsideration on Harbor Village and they succeed, he would have to make a similar attempt for Forest Hills. But if he were to be successful in a move to reconsider Forest Hills, then Manes, Beame,* and Garelik* would all have the problem of taking a position—something they've not yet been called on to do. I'm still convinced that F.H. cannot be legally reconsidered by the Board of Estimate except on a petition from Golar, but that wouldn't be easy to explain to the community.

Friday, June 9, 1972

Carole Lipert,** one of Birbach's people, called. She said that last night at the F.H. Residents Association meeting she was "cruelly booed" when she said that I could be reached; they told her that I was totally unavailable. It's not easy to say why.

Lipert said, "Make it totally a house for the aged—with a geriatric center." She complained last night that the other civic associations had failed to contribute to the F.H.R.A. cause. Birbach has repeatedly said that there are dozens of civic groups and thousands of people across the city supporting him—but they never show up.

Lipert called again later today and we made an appointment.

There was a surprise development in Harbor Village today. Somehow Sam Leone, borough president of Brooklyn, was only able to get Beame and Garelik to go along with him on the vote to reconsider. All the others voted to put the matter off until after the primary. It was a temporary coup for the mayor, but it has

---

* Abraham Beame, then New York city comptroller, now mayor, and Sanford Garelik, then president of the City Council.

** A pseudonym.

apparently put a real wedge between him and Meade Esposito, the Brooklyn Democratic county leader. His whole attack was directed against Leone as "Boss" Meade's puppet.

This doesn't end the problem because eventually a vote will have to be taken, but since it will be postprimary and it's two weeks off, there will be plenty of time for further maneuvering by the pros.

It seems to me clearer and clearer that the mayor is thinking seriously about a third term. He has set about his work with a new vigor since his return from the Florida and Wisconsin debacles. His team has been reconstructed, he is traveling into communities, he has a new ethnic awareness and—maybe most important—he apparently has nowhere else to go. It should be interesting if he runs—all the other potential candidates are dying to know. This could be a real factor here.

My own position with the administration is something of an odd one. I don't blame people generally for thinking that I'm an administration person—after all, the mayor did designate me. And not many people are aware that I've had continuing disagreements with the administration since Willets Point. It's not terribly important except in terms of my usefulness in the present situation. But any misconceptions may be cleared up when (and if) my report is given; I can't imagine reporting fully without some criticism of the manner in which this project was planned.

More F.H.R.A. people have called. They're surprised to learn that they have not been told the truth about my availability. I've made appointments with all of them.

Saturday, June 10, 1972

Corona rejoices!

I received calls most of the morning from our Corona people thanking everybody from God to the governor for signing the compromise bill. There was no negative activity as far as I could see, and if we're very lucky this may mark the end of the six-year war. It certainly would have been awful—with respect to the Forest Hills problem—if the governor hadn't signed the bill and thereby left the high school, which Forest Hills will need more than ever, still up in the air. *Deo gratias.* I hope F.H. will work out nearly as well. It would be something if both of these crushing conundrums could be resolved peacefully, within months of one another.

The Sommos had something to be happy about today, too. The son-in-law was in to see me this morning. Assemblyman Dom DiCarlo's bill was also signed on Friday, which means it will be possible for the Sommos to buy back their home from the city. Elderly and illiterate, they had lost their home to the city by inadvertently failing to pay real estate taxes. The tax obligation was only a fraction of what the house was worth, but until DiCarlo's bill, the law would not have allowed the Sommos to redeem. Now, here's a good deed. Dom DiCarlo spent hours putting his *in Rem* bill together, talking to me, Commissioner of Real Estate Ira Duchan and many others. The bill has been passed, the Sommos will be saved and so will others who get themselves caught up in the incredible bureaucratic labyrinth of the city's *in Rem* delinquency procedure. And not a word of publicity for Dom. Another good man. It's nice to know there are some of these fellows around.

A group from Fr. Pitcaithly's halfway house was in this P.M. They run the night program for addicts in Richmond Hill. They've had trouble with Samaritan House and they're being forced to set up their own program. It's a good group and I'm going to try to get them some free help; they could never raise by themselves the money they need to run the program on a full-time basis. It's a reminder: the housing problem in F.H. is only the tip of the iceberg.

Sunday, June 11, 1972

Mickey Beller and I spent most of the day with a representative of the Housing Authority on a tour of various low- and middle-income projects. We went from Castle Hill in the Bronx to several others in that borough, then to Isaac-Holmes, Ravenswood, Pomonak, Queensbridge, and Latimer Gardens, among others.

The conclusions were almost self-evident. None of the areas surrounding the projects we saw were precisely compatible with F.H. For the most part, these projects were built in slum areas.

Where they weren't, they had no visible effect on the surrounding community. Thus, at Castle Hill, new Mitchell-Lamas and new private residences were built around the project after it was erected. Residents of the area told me they were not greatly affected by any crime problems. Other projects like Queensbridge were so vast that they formed communities of their own and were near disasters.

It also seemed clear that wherever there were large numbers of welfare people the attendant social problems were obvious and difficult to deal with. The projects that worked well, such as Isaac-Holmes, were low welfare and high elderly in composition. I gather that the H.A. itself is painfully aware of this but is limited in what it can do about the problem because of the legal restrictions against screening.

Almost everyone agrees that the 840-unit figure was not a desirable one but that it was compelled by the fiscal aspects of the problem.

Mickey and I both felt that the Housing Authority would welcome an increase of the elderly units to 40 percent of population, which would be 60 percent of the *units*, assuming no other change was made in the size of the project. Golar is by no means intractable on this point.

Earlier in the day I had been to the Cunningham Apartments in Queens where there are now 40 percent black and about 15 percent welfare as a result of the H.A.'s leasing program. The rest are white lower-middle income. It's a privately owned development.

When we lived at Cunningham about ten years ago, it was entirely white and mostly Jewish with no low-income. It was then only about fifteen years old, but the highly transient population had already left indelible scars. The apartments were a way station between the rapidly deteriorating Brooklyn and South Queens areas and a heavily mortgaged Cape Cod in a "better" community. The development now appears to me no worse kept than it was ten years ago.

The blacks I spoke to this morning all felt that the welfare cases were the problem and that without them scatter-site could work. But scatter-site is *for* them as much as for anyone.

Monday, June 12, 1972

The calls from F.H.R.A. people continue and Birbach continues to say publicly we are not communicating with them. Most seem to realize that a "compromise" of some kind should be worked toward. Many appear to be awaiting the results of the Birbach–Gold race.

I spoke to Herbert Kahn. His group, the Queens Council for Better Housing, which has fought for the project for the past six years, has taken the position that the entire idea of an independent fact-finder or "mediator" is evil. He seems to feel that any compromise would be illegal. I told Kahn that he appeared to be as close-minded as Birbach. His "justification" was that he has been in the matter longer.

I told Kahn that even if his group refused to recognize the idea of my role, I would like to have the benefit of his ideas "off the record." I pushed him on this and he wasn't prepared for it. He didn't say no and promised to get back to me. I don't think he will.

Kahn's people, and many others, have a heavy emotional investment in the project. Since the beginning they have struggled selflessly for what they took to be an unchallengeable good. It is hard for them to see the opposition as being anything but bigoted and racist. They have developed the crusader's intolerance and it will be difficult if not impossible to talk rationally with them.

Tuesday, June 13, 1972

It's nearly 2 A.M. and it would probably be wiser to sleep, but so much was said tonight I felt it should be put down while it was still fresh. I had nearly seven hours at Borough Hall and for the most part, I was on the listening end.

The first group consisted of four people—two middle-aged couples. The Gordons* have been residents for twenty-seven years within blocks of the project site. The Steins** are tenants who

* A pseudonym.
** A pseudonym.

belong to the F.H.R.A. Gordon is a retired schoolteacher and came prepared with a full set of lecture notes. He tried hard to be coolly professional in his delivery, but before long he was caught up in his own fear and wound up literally screaming at me. There was no devil's advocate role possible with him; any probing question that appeared contradictory of his position was pure "devil" and no advocate. He recited the entire litany of arguments against the project; its ignoble genesis, a borough president who "sold them out," a land "scheme" by Muss, the "phony liberal" concept, the density, and finally, the real issue—crime. There was no shaking his belief that welfare and increased crime are inseparable. He finished up in a crescendo—"My wife will be mugged and raped and you ask me to be reasonable!" He feels—and I'm sure he's sincere— that no project that permits any welfare families can be tolerated. He also mentioned the possible depreciation of his property values.

Fear—that's what Gordon was all about. How do you argue with it?

It seems clear to me that the influx of welfare families will bring with it a threat of increased crime. That has been checked out in several sources and is a matter of almost common experience. Retired Captain of the Police Force Frank Krupp, verified it again at the end of the night. But if it *is* true where does that leave us? Is it better to keep these families and their crime in the ghetto, where crime is already rampant? Gordon, Grunblatt, and Lashinsky, who were in later, think so. "Why spoil the good?" they say. Krupp agreed. He seems a fair and intelligent man with thirty years of experience with crime in the city generally, and some experience with project areas particularly. He feels that crime in the project is inevitable, and even increased police protection won't help much. He had harrowing stories to tell about the elderly in some Bronx projects.

Martin Garner, an Elmhurst resident, came in with a prepared paper. He recommended scaling down to half size, then taking half of this for middle-income and the balance for elderly low-income. He regards the cost as irrelevant, given the damage the project could do if permitted to remain as it is now.

Benjamin Elterman of the Jewish War Veterans wants the project ditched and a veterans' facility built in its place.

The American Jewish Congress came in with three representatives. They wish their position to be off the record until a compromise is adopted, if one ever is. I talked to them generally about the mix possibilities and they felt something along those lines would be a good idea. But they are powerfully noncommittal and prefer the back seat, at least for the time being.

Lashinsky, Rabbi Grunblatt, and Katzberg were in together. Lashinsky appears to me virtually immovable. He's convinced the project is a direct and deliberate attack on the Jews.

Grunblatt was a rabbi tonight. He was prepared, analytical, and articulate. Overall he was fair except that some of his Talmudic references were terribly strained in their application to the F.H. situation. He is perhaps more significant as a community leader than anyone else in F.H. His temple, almost directly across from the project, has a congregation of about one thousand.

Again—the fear of crime. His bottom line: 100 percent for the elderly, preferably with reduced buildings.

Grunblatt, like the other rabbis, appears to be under a great personal strain. His religious orientation, with all of its ancient emphasis on love and altruism, must be squared with his position against the project. He has decided upon what he regards as good sense and a loyalty to his own flock, but I don't think it's been easy.

Lashinsky thought no portion of the project would be salable as a Mitchell-Lama because of the stigma attached to it by the publicity this situation has received.

We have agreed to meet again on the twenty-first.

Krupp was helpful again. He has an interesting slant on police security problems and its relationship to architecture. He supplied me with a great deal of information that I'll read tomorrow. He suggested that from a security point of view it would be best to have all the elderly in one building. This is being done in the new Pruitt Igoe development in St. Louis. There are other opinions, however; some feel that this would make the elderly easy prey for deviants and the like.

Dr. Newman at N.Y.U. is still in the process of preparing a

detailed study of high rises and the incidence of crime. I understand it will confirm Krupp's position.

Another recurrent theme tonight was the difficulty of assuring any effective screening process. The opponents to the project are well aware of the legal limitations on the power to screen tenants and it increases their apprehension. They know, for example, that the H.A. is not even able to get Police Department records as to arrests or drug addiction. This is another illustration of the necessity to balance competing considerations. No doubt there is a danger in circulating arrest records; it presents a threat to civil rights. But then there is undeniable validity in making intelligent choices of tenants—for the safety of the project as well as the community. Surely, with some thought, a way could be found to serve both ends here.

Wednesday, June 14, 1973

This was the busiest, toughest and most discouraging day so far. I met with Golar from 2:00 until about 5:30, checked at City Hall for some information on Electchester, another abortive project in Queens, and finished up at Borough Hall after midnight.

Golar's position overall is that he will surrender no low-income housing units without replacing them somewhere in Queens County. With this in mind, we had a good deal of talk concerning Electchester, and I agreed that I would look into the possibility of reviving the mixed middle-income/low-income project there. This presents an obvious problem; the sure reaction from the community will be that we are permitting the "blight" to spread.

Golar points to Latimer Gardens, a low-income housing project in Flushing, Queens, as an example of the scatter-site program and uses it as a precedent.

He points out that 15 percent of the entire city population is welfare and that percentage is hardly exceeded in public housing. This is strikingly inconsistent. The housing program is supposed to assist the most needy. Welfare are the most needy, and yet the percentage of welfare in housing projects is at the same ratio that welfare is to the entire population above them. Golar uses this point to emphasize that the Forest Hills project will not be flooded by welfare, and that this, by itself, is a great concession to the community.

He insists that he does not have a bad project in a middle-class area. This, of course, is the heart of the matter, as was to be confirmed later in the day.

Golar has often stated that public housing ought not to be labeled as such and certainly ought never to be described in terms of "low-income." He would opt for a middle-income/low-income mix wherever possible. I pressed him on this point, suggesting that the 236 idea was at least a step in that direction; but he quickly countered with the absolute necessity of replacing any of the 840 units with low-income units elsewhere in Queens.

There is nothing surprising about Golar's position. He is treating this matter as though it were a commercial lawsuit. At the moment he has "won" 840 units. Unless the Forest Hills' forces prevail in the Court of Appeals, or the Board of Estimate were to decide to reconsider, there is no apparent way in which this number can be reduced, so why give up any units?

Golar was well prepared for the idea of cutting down the project physically. He had tentative figures which indicated three floors might be lopped off without any city monies. But these were subject to being checked. Golar reported that the piling was going well. I had checked that independently and was given the same information.

Golar said that the percentage of elderly could conceivably be increased. I told him that if it could be gotten up to where the Isaacs-Holmes Project was, it would certainly sweeten the project as far as Forest Hills was concerned, although there was no reason to believe that it would satisfy the community at this point.

I suggested the possibility of putting all the elderly in one building for security purposes, and Golar said he did not think it could be done because of the design problems. I'll check that out myself.

With respect to the Section 23 leasing program,* which subsi-

---

* Section 23 of the Housing and Development Act of 1965, permits the New York City Housing Authority to lease standard units in privately owned buildings and to

dizes rent payments for low-income tenants in existing private middle-income apartment houses, Golar said that he had used up his specific allocation and did not think this approach would be helpful. This is something else that we ought to check out with H.U.D.

My trip to City Hall was nonproductive. Kriegel was in the middle of a dozen things, and the most I could do was to ask that he have someone gather whatever materials he had on Electchester.

The first group in tonight at Borough Hall, was put together by Peter Ferguson, acting director of the New York Urban League's Operation Open City. They were about a dozen people, representing Rochdale Health Center, Citizens' Committee of Flushing, Long Island City Housing Services; Flushing N.A.A.C.P., Women's Strike for Peace, Bellpark Vets for Peace, Queens Liberal Party, and a professional men's league. From what I've been able to gather up to this point this group is fairly representative of the groups that support the project. For the most part, they're not residents of the community and aren't immediately affected. It's fair to say that it's easier for these groups to operate from high "moral" precepts. Many of the individuals can recite previous residence in Forest Hills or past personal experiences with projects, but their present platform is from a geographical point sufficiently remote from the site to be free of whatever threat may be inherent in the project.

Their arguments run approximately as follows:

1. This project has been passed upon by the Board of Estimate, the courts and the Legislature. There is no justification now for reducing or in any way altering it because the system has operated

---

sublease these apartments to low-income persons eligible for public housing. At the time of the Forest Hills situation, 30 percent of the total federal contribution to the city for housing purposes was required to be used for leased housing. Such leasing could involve new construction or existing housing. Tenants would pay the same rental as for comparable housing in public projects. The federal government, under this program, makes contributions to the Housing Authority in the form of annual cash subsidies, which enable the Authority to pay the difference between the market rent and the rent paid by tenants. Section 23 leasing may be used with Mitchell-Lama and Section 236.

fully. Indeed, Herbert Kahn's group has threatened to bring legal action should there be any movement toward change at all. They regard the Board of Estimate's resolution as a "mandate."

2. The scatter-site concept is good. It means taking people out of the ghettos and giving them a better place to live. (But is this so? The experience of projects in slum areas is that they run themselves down terribly and are eventually replaced by other similar projects. Will it be different in F.H.? And mightn't there be a better way?)

3. The size cannot be altered because we need as many units as possible to permit the blacks, particularly, to generate an economic strength that will allow the creation of commercial facilities for themselves as part of the project complex. (Tyrone Stallings of the N.A.A.C.P. made this point and I talked to him some about it. I felt that it sounded as though it ran counter to the integration theory and was more consistent with the Black Nationalists' approach. Some of the other speakers later withdrew from it completely.)

Joan Rosenthal and some other F.H. residents were also in to support the project. Joan and her friends had fought us for five years in Corona, but she is pleasant and easy to get along with.

All of the proponents argue from almost purely moral and theoretical grounds. Indeed, none, other than Golar, have pointed out that by virtue of court decisions scatter-site is virtually compelled as a matter of law. The argument for, as presented by most of these people, is constructed of noble and appealing generalizations on the visceral and the surface equities. The plight of the black, the rest of the community's moral obligation, the tradition to aid the downtrodden—that's how the case is being made. But beneath the apparent equities and based on the evidence the question is not so clear. Is it provable that this will be good for the downtrodden? What effects will it have in terms of economic integration? Will its size result in insularizing this group and effectively creating an independent separate community, thereby defeating the objective of integration? And what effect will it have on the neighboring community? If apartments in neighboring buildings begin to show increasing vacancies, won't that result in landlords filling the space with welfare, thereby eventually spreading the welfare and low-income community throughout? Logically progressed, mightn't this result in the welfare city that some accused Lindsay of wanting years ago? And would that be good?

The last wave in was perhaps the best equipped of the opponents. Three or four lawyers were included in a group of about twenty or thirty F.H.R.A. members. The arguments were the familiar ones, and except for a single person who was willing to consider a project totally for the elderly the others said the project in any form would be objectionable and they would move. At about midnight I took this tack with them: "I have been assigned to ascertain whether a compromise can be found that would be reasonably acceptable to both sides. That is the whole of my mandate. If, therefore, the city will not, or cannot, consider killing the project entirely, I am left simply with the alternative of reporting that there is no point in attempting to reduce or alter the project in any way because it would do nothing for the F.H. people." They were distressed at the way I put it and I think they felt it was a threat, but since they had no opportunity to consult with one another no one was willing to state any reaction. I decided to leave them with the thought and agreed to talk to them again next week.

It is increasingly clear that the F.H.R.A. is trying to flood me by making appointments in separate smaller groups, thereby getting multiple opportunities at me. While time becomes the real problem with each passing day, I'll continue to meet with as many as I can. After all, they are principal among the antagonists.

The nightly sessions at Borough Hall are running from 6 P.M. until approximately midnight. We've insisted upon appointments but each night a few people show up at the conference room without having checked first. If they're willing to wait until the end of the discussions with those who were calendared, I talk to these people as well. Attendance has been terrific; the lines outside the Hall make the place look like a busy doctor's waiting room. I should be so lucky!

Thursday, June 15, 1972

My birthday. I celebrated it by spending most of the day at the office speaking with callers on F.H. Tonight I traveled out to a Democratic Club in Brooklyn where I addressed the group for about twenty minutes. I said very little and it was fairly well received. If I had tried to say something meaningful they probably would have ignored me—it was the "eve of election" and hardly a time to be thinking. I went principally so that I could talk to City Councilman Monroe Cohen and some of the other leaders about Harbor Village. Cohen is expecting to lose his attempt at reconsideration before the Board of Estimate on the twenty-second. He thinks Manes will back away because he doesn't want to have to recall F.H. and possibly even Parkway Village. I need to anticipate the effect of the Harbor Village decision on our situation.

Friday, June 16, 1972

Commissioner Eleanor Norton* reached me by phone today. Golar and the mayor had apparently asked her to get in touch with me. She probably wouldn't have done it on her own, but I think my telling Golar that all the black home owners I've talked to are opposed has stimulated him into getting me some other voices. I told Commissioner Norton the same thing and she will probably get me more blacks. Norton did not like the idea of the number of the elderly being increased until I suggested that if the percentage of low-income black elderly was much higher than white, we could help put an end to the "bigot" argument by introducing an even higher percentage of blacks (by increasing the number of elderly) than would be in the project as presently designed. This is sound theoretically; the difficulty is that historically most elderly low-income are white and it might be legally impossible to arrange for a predominantly black elderly population.

Tonight I went to Jeantet's restaurant to meet Joe DeVoy at

---

* Then commissioner of the New York City Human Rights Commission.

8:30. I waited nearly an hour and he didn't show. I'll call him Monday to find out what happened.

I spent the morning trying to keep my practice afloat. Since I've never spent any substantial amount of time away from the office, the clients aren't accustomed to my being unavailable—and I have been unavailable for most of the past four weeks. I'll have to do something.

I was at the "other" Forest Hills from five to eight at the Goldstones' cocktail party. As a group they're about equally divided on the 108th Street project.

The Forest Hills Gardens people are the elite. They are very well off and highly educated. This makes their cocktail parties generally things to be avoided; the competition gets to be terrific after a few martinis. The Gardens people I've come to know in the past several months are, however, unusually easy to get along with. Overall, I think most of them favor a project at 108th Street in some reduced form. As their attorney in the Lefrak case, where we have so far successfully stopped a luxury high rise,* I've told them it would be better for them not to get involved publicly in the 108th Street dispute. But they've been helpful with ideas and information. Lyn Quigley went to the trouble of digging out her Harvard thesis on the architecture of residences for the elderly. I read it through, and it supplied me with a great deal that was valuable with respect to the elderly in this low-income project.

I spent the evening with Breslin. At about midnight we went out to East New York and saw a project that has been in construction for about seven years. We talked to some of the blacks in the area, and were it not for their recognition of J.B. I don't think we would have gotten much from them. In any event they were more intent in talking about their Block Association, which seemed to be working very well, than 108th Street. They regard the 108th Street Project as academic and certainly not something to get excited about.

Breslin was himself—he seems even more intent on arriving at a solution to the F.H. situation than I am. His seriousness and

* In May of 1973 the Court of Appeals decided 4 to 3 to permit the construction.

relentlessness are things I've come to take for granted. I suspect his public would be terribly disillusioned if they knew this about him.

Sunday, June 18, 1973

Three or four hours of reading, including Jane Jacobs' book on the cities. The rest of the day was spent trying to catch up on various firm work. I wish I didn't have to make a living—it would leave time for so many more worthwhile things!

I came across something in my research today that was particularly interesting. In 1966—January 10, to be precise—a group headed by Charles Abrams and including people like Ed Logue and I. D. Robbins reported to Mayor Lindsay on housing and urban renewal.* This was at the very outset of the Lindsay administration and months before Corona and Forest Hills were moved through the City Planning Commission and the Board of Estimate.

The report clearly noted that the mayor's housing policy ought to provide for racial and income diversity throughout the city. In effect it called for "scatter-site" housing. It also cautioned that the city ought to listen attentively to the community's own ideas. It stated that whatever projects were constructed by way of an attempt at racial dispersal, the buildings should be designed so as to fit in neatly "as part of existing neighborhoods" and should not "massively be superimposed on them."

The report also recommended in passing that cooperative arrangements be considered.

One has to wonder whether this report was ever read or considered by the mayor and the people in charge of his housing policy. A look back now indicates that the suggestions set forth in the report were either not heard or simply not heeded. My guess is that the report effectively disappeared immediately upon being filed. The more I get into the files and the writings upon this whole subject the more I am convinced that much of the cumulative

---

* Report of the Housing and Urban Renewal Task Force to Mayor John V. Lindsay, January 10, 1966.

intelligence that has been produced by numerous individuals and groups has been left completely unmined; commissions are created, reports are prepared and filed and that's the end of it. The press of business, bureaucratic neglect, and lack of continuity in offices dooms many of these efforts to fruitlessness. In the City-State Commission* we produced numbers of papers and even "studies of studies," and aside from those of us who worked on the problems, I suspect few, if any, profited from the research and conclusions. We are always, it seems, starting from scratch when in fact much of the thinking has already been done.

Monday, June 19, 1972

It is clear now that the burden of trying to talk with all of those who wish to present their position will make it impossible to meet the original six-week deadline. Hal Levenson was right. While communication and a measuring of the sentiments of the parties involved were essential, the vast amount of time consumed by the process has made it difficult to do everything else that needs to be done. Beginning next week we'll be able to see only "leaders." Within the next ten days we must have at least a rough concept of a compromise if there is to be one. Without it it would be difficult to talk meaningfully with the federal and state officials. Eventually we'll need to get their reaction and help with respect to a specific proposal—and what we need, therefore, *is* a specific proposal. And all the while, the work continues at the site; time is a real enemy.

While crossing Queens Boulevard on the way to the Borough Hall Building tonight, I was nearly struck by a car occupied by five well-dressed gentlemen, with a bumper that bore two large "Birbach Team" signs. I'm sure it was inadvertent—I hope it was inadvertent! Ten minutes later the occupants, who apparently hadn't seen me, walked into the conference room and announced that they were Sidney Bloom** and company from Forest Hills.

* The New York City Commission on city-state affairs of which William Vanden Heuvel was chairman and the author a member.
** A pseudonym.

My first question was whether they were members of Birbach's organization. At first they were inclined to deny it. Like all the other dozens of Forest Hills Residents Association members who have been in to see me they were either afraid it would be prejudicial to admit the association or they were pursuing a deliberate plan to inundate me. They are willing to take advantage of the opportunity to make their points but don't want to have their organization committed. They're trying very hard to eat their cake and have it too. I can't say I disagree with their tactics, given their skepticism about my involvement. In fact, if I were counseling them I'd probably advise them to do precisely what they're doing. As long as I'm aware of it, it won't hurt.

The arguments they made were the traditional ones. In effect, what they said was that the low-income people would eventually deteriorate the neighborhood as they had Crown Heights and other Jewish communities. I put to them the flat question whether they wished me to report that unless the entire project was "killed" there would be no acceptable compromise. I asked them about the possibility of recomposing the project so that it would be predominantly elderly. They wanted time to consider and to get back to me. They've been well tutored.

Another group of F.H.R.A. members—all of them women—were next. They were extremely antagonistic in the beginning, and as a matter of fact, I was sharp with two of them. They'd been filled with phony stories about Corona and had all sorts of preconceptions about my "political" affiliation. Their arguments were less sophisticated than others I've heard. They felt that people who had not worked for it should not be given "expensive" apartments. They felt that they had been conspired against by an anti-Jewish mayor. They resented the fact that Corona Italians had "fought off" the project. I pointed out to them that it was not the Corona people who moved the project at all. But they simply refused to listen, let alone believe. They swore they would all move out if the project in any form were to be built. "Do you really mean you would want me to report that the project should remain as is unless it could be undone completely?" They softened—but only a bit.

The best they would do is to consider all elderly, and at that, the buildings would have to be drastically cut down.

Nash Kestenbaum, president of the National Young Israel movement, Rabbi Lauer, and Dr. Felix Glaubach, also of Young Israel, were in at 9:30. Kestenbaum is regarded as one of the principal spokesmen for the Orthodox Jews who oppose the project. He is intensely dedicated, almost fiercely so. He makes a powerful presentation—rapid fire, brow knit, eyes aflame. Listening to him and watching him I could see how little chance the Arabs have. He's good. He started with an inaccurate history of the project and I corrected him with respect to the involvement of the Corona people and, for that matter, the Forest Hills people, in the early years. Kestenbaum made the following points:

1. Even if the fear of the people were unjustified, the very fact of its existence should be enough to require a change in the project.

2. Certain black groups, like, CORE and NEGRO are against the project but have not said so publicly.

3. Even the N.A.A.C.P. supports the project only because of a commitment to integration and not because it regards the project itself as good.

Kestenbaum's alternative solution was a six-story garden apartment exclusively for the elderly. He argued that this would be the only way to ensure the success of scatter-site housing in the future. I made the point that if the project were limited to the elderly, there would be no way to get other communities to accept low-income families—who are the source of the real problem—in any form of dispersal. No response from Kestenbaum.

Tuesday, June 20, 1972

Primary Day. It's going to be an interesting one. As a matter of pure logic, it shouldn't make much difference whether Birbach or Gold wins. Unless there is a very strong vote against Gold in the Forest Hills area itself it would be difficult to ascribe any significance to the election in terms of the community sentiment on the project. As a practical matter, a strong Gold victory would probably be interpreted by the community at large (including the many groups interested in the Forest Hills situation) as a strong indication that compromise is feasible. It won't make any real difference to me.

Today started at 9:30 A.M. with Haskell Lazere of the American Jewish Committee. Lazere had no substantial contribution to make with respect to a compromise solution but did say that his committee was working on a program along the lines of the Neighbors' approach which would be designed to assist in the attempt to make the project (whatever its form) workable. Things like an educational program, community guidance clinic, PAL chapter, etc. The program would be highly formalized under the sponsorship of a community group. Lazere, personally, is certainly amenable to compromise but felt that the committee might be reluctant to give support. They're afraid the issue is too controversial. He suggested the possibility of an elderly low-income Mitchell-Lama, and pure low-income respectively, in the three 24-story towers. He said that some female housing expert had given him the idea, but that she did not want her name revealed. Lazere agreed to have this woman submit to me a more detailed description of her plan, anonymously.

Later this morning Rabbi Bruce Cole, Seymour Reich of the Queens Chapter of the B'nai B'rith-ADL and Bob Koehler, New York regional director of the B'nai B'rith Anti-Defamation League, appeared. They started by favoring a cutting down of the buildings. Koehler had thought it through and felt that the original expenditure by the city would be made up in the long run by reduced maintenance costs, greater efficiency and increased success potential for the project itself. Koehler was also strong on the Neighbors' approach. Reich, in making the argument for reducing the buildings pointed out that statistics showed high-rise buildings were not the best suited for low-income families, and particularly the elderly, although they might be for the luxury category. This group also thought they could support any reasonable compromise. They didn't react warmly to the suggestion of a Mitchell-Lama in one of the three 24-story towers and keeping the other two intact but making them predominantly for the elderly.

This meeting, like practically all of them so far, was cordial and, I think, candid. It's a shame that so much of this good feeling will probably be dissipated in the dissatisfaction with the eventual report: no matter what the report, there will be dissatisfaction.

Tonight in Borough Hall, I met with the Coordinating Committee of the Parents Associations of the local elementary schools. Four women were present; they were all Forest Hills residents, and all were opposed to the project. They proposed what they regarded as a perfect solution—move the school from Corona to 108th Street and forget about the project. They were fully armed with the facts and statistics concerning the insufficiency of services. These were four refined, well-intentioned women, none of whom had any firm grasp of the underlying history and actual facts of the present situation. Practically every night one is reminded of how imperfect our system is with regard to communicating facts. Dozens of misconceptions have been generated and are fervently believed and brandished by people involved in this controversy. It's difficult to tell whether this is the result of intellectual slippage, the efficacy of the demagogues, or a simple fabrication by the people involved. But if they are fabrications, then I've met some of the best actors in New York City outside of the Broadway stage. I'm more inclined to believe that most of these people are sincere and for some reason have just suspended, in the present context, their normal analytical and intellectual abilities. This is particularly curious, since most of them appear to be skeptical people who would not normally believe anything without hard proof. Perhaps they've simply concluded that politicians are inveterate liars and, therefore, one can safely believe as a fact anything that contradicts a "political" statement. In any event, it's made the dialogue extremely difficult.

Wednesday, June 21, 1972

All morning at the Horn-Halliburton Board of Directors meeting. But Forest Hills is unavoidable. I was ten minutes late for the meeting, and the first thing I was asked about by our friends from Texas was how things were going in Forest Hills. There was apparently some reference made to it, in *Time* or *Newsweek*, which they picked up.

I've been fortunate in the cooperation and understanding I've received from most of our clients. Although a few have already been irreparably offended by their inability to reach me easily, for the most part the clients are bearing with it. Some of them—like Horn Construction—have even offered assistance. Their vast expertise has been made freely available to me. While this is partially explicable by our long and solid relationship, their sensitivity to the implications of this problem has also moved them. The situation has brought out the worst in many people, but it's also shown the good and solid instincts in many others.

Many of those objecting to the project point to the inadequacy of services in the area—schools, transportation, etc.—and say that without adequate services there should be no project. City representatives have said that Forest Hills is well equipped in terms of all essential and auxiliary services. The fact is that practically no part of the city is really adequately equipped. It would follow that no part of the city can accept any new project. Planners and sociologists suggest that before a project is built, the services ought to be beefed up. But how does one do this? Is it possible to find more money and more policemen for this area and to build a subway line, and to reduce the census in the local schools? And if it were possible, why shouldn't it be done without respect to whether a project was going to be built?

So the Forest Hills Neighbors ask for increased police, a personal environmental survey by Jerry Kretchmer,* an investigation of all local buildings by the Building Department to correct violations, and a survey of the transportation facilities in the area by some city official. The idea of attempting to marshal the city forces to squeeze out whatever few additional services are available for the Forest Hills area in order to assist the community in carrying the load of the project is a good one, however limited the possibilities. Why not recommend an all-agencies meeting and a

---

* Jerome Kretchmer, chairman of the Environmental Protection Administration at the time.

coordinator of services? At least the suggestion will be noncontroversial.

I asked the Neighbors to prepare a paper and to get it to me.

One thing suggested by Paul Sandman of the Neighbors group troubled me. He felt that the attitude of the Forest Hills residents had to be changed. More specifically, instead of thinking of welfare tenants as numbers and abstractions, they should be thought of as human beings. To accomplish this he wants to escort the people of Forest Hills to various projects. I shudder to think of the reaction they would have to Queensbridge and some of the other projects I've seen.

I told Sandman I had mentioned the "cooperative" idea to Golar and that I would get back to him on it. I've been giving it a great deal of thought and study, and it still seems that the legal impediments are substantial.

Lashinsky, Seymour Samuels, some sociologists, Rabbi Grunblatt and others were the second wave tonight. One sociologist, a professor emeritus from Rutgers, was refreshingly reasonable. He talked about the possibility of a Mitchell-Lama mix. I spent a great deal of time arguing against (more devil than advocate) the idea of making the project totally for the elderly. The sociologist agreed that it would be virtually impossible to sell low-income families to any middle-income area if none were placed at 108th Street. Grunblatt talked about scaling down, and when I suggested that his idea of reducing the project to six stories was probably "not salable," he indicated, without stating so flatly, that a reduction to twelve stories might be reasonable.

Seymour Samuels is smooth, affable, and ostensibly frank. I asked him directly about the announcement that the Queens Jewish Community Council had set up its own group to study compromise, and whether they would cooperate with our effort. He was evasive at first. But when I pressed him, he said that their judgment was that I might very well have already made an agreement with the mayor, and for that reason they were going to prepare a recommendation which they would hold until after my report and then use as their response. Samuels said, in effect, that because they could not trust me, they did not wish me to know what they were working on. He also told me that Don Manes was aware of their intentions. That bothered me, since I would have expected Don to talk to me about the situation had he known of it.

At that point I shed whatever diplomatic restraint I've been able to clothe myself with, and told Samuels that I regarded him and his group as insulting. I told him I objected to his involving himself with me on repeated occasions only in order to feed himself and his organization without any intention of reciprocating. I also told him very plainly that I thought he had a hell of a nerve suggesting that I was involved in some kind of elaborate pretense. Although this was done partly for effect, I confess I came very close to losing my cool. I found it nearly infuriating after all these days and nights to hear Samuels say I was "conspiring" against them. But then, perhaps some good may come of it. We'll see how they react.

Earlier in the discussion, Samuels indicated that the project should be cut down 50 percent. Samuels also said that he did not like the idea of the Mitchell-Lama mix because after the first wave the project would be filled up with welfare people.

Rabbi Grunblatt is realistic. He pointed out that there are only two questions left: size and composition. On size, I believe he would settle for half. On composition, he would need to have at least 70 percent elderly with an assurance that it would remain elderly.

The next group was the Ethical Culture group. They favor the project as is: they feel 840 units are minimum. They would be shocked at any compromise and refuse to recognize an exodus as a possibility. These are nice people of the highest type.

The last group were made up of resident opponents led by Rabbi Ross, a gentle, pleasant leader of Temple Sinai, which I understand is a Reform temple. He recited his experiences in Chicago and elsewhere in this city where he claims the intrusion of welfare families gradually deteriorated the community, so that he was forced to move. He made a strong argument for the Jewish community's right to preserve its identity and integrity. He feels this right is being violated by the intrusion of this "colossal" project. He thinks the extent of the fear is such that *any* number of low-income people will destroy this community by chasing his people out. He treats their fear as the critical factor to be contended with.

A college professor and a "planner" were part of Rabbi Ross's group, and they submitted a compromise proposal in writing. It operated from the premise that the community should have absolute control over tenant selection. I pointed out that I thought this was not legally feasible because of Circuit Court of Appeals rulings. Their suggestion was that a moratorium be declared until the case could be brought to the Supreme Court.

Meg Katz finished up, and she was in excellent form. She is still a strikingly handsome woman. Her eyes shine and sparkle along with her vigorous prose. She has been slamming me with it (but sometimes almost affectionately) for more than a year in connection with the Corona situation. Made cynical by years of battling politicians she was convinced that I was getting something "under the table" for my efforts. She arrived at this conclusion because she felt that doing it for nothing was not reasonable. She reminded me that she still believed I had "sold out" the people of Corona, although she had not yet been able to prove what I had received from Mayor Lindsay by way of compensation. Her entire argument—which was quite eloquently stated—centered on the proposition that the middle class was being destroyed. She felt that the only acceptable position would be a strong stand against the entire project, forcing the mayor by moral and public pressure to abandon the whole idea. She said that the man who made such a recommendation could be mayor. She pointed to the Baisley Park Project which she claims was rejected by the blacks, and she says that there is no strong support from the black community for this project. She may be right on this latter point, particularly with respect to Baisley Park.

The density argument and all the traditional attacks upon projects are repeated each night. Invariably, mention of the failure of a meaningful hearing before now is also repeated. These are fairly legitimate arguments, which have been voiced by many in the city for a long time. They are heightened here by the intense fear generated by the project.

Emotionally, it would be easy to conclude against the opponents and to strike down, therefore, all of their arguments. But that would be dishonest. Regardless of one's ultimate conclusion about the wisdom and efficacy of the proposed complex, one would necessarily have to find truth and some intelligence on both sides of the argument. The temptation to be simplistic is always present— it's easier to deal in absolutes.

Thursday, June 22, 1972

State Senator Emanuel Gold called, and I arranged to meet with him Saturday morning. He said that the latest figures indicated his victory over Birbach was even more substantial than he had originally expected.

A former member of the Forest Hills Residents Association called. He's eager to sit down—and I agreed to meet with him Monday night, the twenty-sixth. He had resigned from the F.H.R.A. when he got tired of their style. He claims that Birbach cut me up every chance he got and told his people that I had been offered a judgeship, was being paid surreptitiously and had "sold out" to Lindsay a long time ago. My old friend Jerry! I was gratified and surprised to learn, however, that many people, even in the F.H.R.A., didn't believe these charges. I'm surprised because I'm a stranger to most of these people, and on the face of the situation the contentions are not improbable ones.

Birbach was quoted as having said he would resign from the F.H.R.A. if he lost the election. I'm sure he won't. The situation reminds me of the Corona battle, where the opponents of compromise kept retreating but were always able to find some contention that would keep them in the public spotlight. I think Jerry is much too taken with his new identity to quit.

Perhaps the most significant call of the day came from John Miller,* formerly with the Department of City Planning. This young man has spent the last four months working on the Forest Hills problem while preparing a thesis at MIT. He gave me some ideas that were extremely interesting and he's agreed to fly down from Boston to meet with me Saturday.

* A pseudonym.

Late afternoon Birbach called. I guessed right. Although it was reported he had previously said he would resign as president of F.H.R.A. if he lost the election, he has no intention of doing so. He's planning a meeting tonight at which he will announce that from this point forward he will fight harder than ever. He's completely caught up in the political game. He refuses to believe that he could have been beaten honestly, and he says that he is putting together a New York City coalition of middle-income people "of all races and creeds" that will sweep into office in 1973. I must conclude that no compromise for which he is not principally responsible will receive anything but his vigorous opposition, at least at first. The situation is almost precisely the same as that in Corona. Jerry was coy about suggesting any compromise and indicated that he would talk to me only if I specifically invited him. I told him that he had long ago received the same invitation that everyone else had. But I think he would like something formal that he could make a point of. He hinted broadly that his grand plan would call for a garden apartment for the elderly with a geriatric center. We had some general discussion concerning the numerous F.H.R.A. members who had been in to see me, and he insisted that they were not speaking for the association. I told him that in any event it was clear that I had spoken with a very large number of its members and had received their views. Jerry said that while his people had reported to him that I was "knowledgeable" and "clever," they were not sure I was not playing some kind of political game with Lindsay. I told him his compliments sounded like insults and that there was really no point in my trying to fight the phantoms they were creating. In any event, Jerry said he would like to get back to me after the meeting tonight.

Captain Krupp showed up promptly at 9:30, and after chatting with him a bit, he was joined by Dr. Katz and the Forest Hills Crescent Group, as well as by Herman Weingard, Rabbi Goldman of the Utopia Jewish Center and Sarah Schwartz, also of the Center. This was another hard-core opposition group, and at the outset they would not consider any alternative.

The arguments were those that have been repeated so often.

At the end of the night, Krupp and I discussed the progress of this process and he noted the pattern of approach which I've been using from the beginning. It seemed to me that the first problem was to persuade each of the parties to this controversy that there was some intelligent reason for relaxing their absolutist stance. It would have been too much to expect that the opposing sides would have agreed to relent simply because they felt that it was charitable and good to sacrifice some portion of their demands in the interest of harmony and peace. Ever since Eve bit the apple and seduced poor Adam, that kind of expectation has been unrealistic. Something harder and more practically compelling is needed.

And so I've listened, night after night, to the opponents and have permitted them to spell out their arguments in great detail. Indeed, I've encouraged and enhanced their arguments in the early stages of each discussion. But then, before the end of our meeting I explain that I'm operating as a devil's advocate and argue the other side of the case. I have reason to believe (and Krupp, who is himself an opponent, agreed) that my argument has at least given some of the opposition pause. I've pointed out to them as clearly as I could—without letting my voice rise to the advocacy pitch—that they have these things to contend with:

1. The political strength of the other side of the issue. That there is no reason to believe that a citywide referendum would favor the Forest Hills position. People not immediately affected are attracted by the presentations of the proponents. The generous instinct to do something for the lowly poor is easier to accommodate from a distance. They (the residents) tend to see Forest Hills as the whole city, and that's short-sighted.

2. The reality of the federal requirement that scatter-site be implemented. It's fine to attack the merits of the proposition, but as a matter of hard law, the city has virtually no alternative now but to attempt to implement the scatter-site concept in some respectable measure.

3. The fact that, for better or for worse, the system has operated fully with respect to the Forest Hills controversy. They have had their opportunity to be heard at the Board of Estimate and the City Planning Commission and in the courts and the Legislature, and they've lost. The idea of undoing what has been done is abhorrent

to many on the simple thesis that the setting aside of a five-year governmental process because the affected group is unhappy with the result might create a precedent that logically extended would lead to chaos.

4. That, in fact, they had their "day in court" and blew it. I reminded them that for two and a half years Forest Hills opposed Corona's suggestion that the new Queens high school be moved to 108th Street to replace the project.

5. That the idea of absolute community control, while superficially appealing, cannot work in this city. Obviously, were each community, like Forest Hills, to have the last word on public projects within its boundaries, public projects and, therefore, city life would be almost totally stultified. Where would one build a methadone clinic, or a halfway house, or a storage plant or a power plant or a bus depot, or a school—or a housing project? With relatively few exceptions, anything requiring some discomfort on the part of the community would be rejected, human nature being, as it is, basically selfish. In short, total decentralization of governmental power in this city is neither wise nor practicable.

6. The need for better conditions for the lowly poor. Ask one of the well-groomed mothers from Forest Hills to put themselves in the place of a husbandless, black welfare mother with three children, living in a hovel in the midst of a ghetto that is pure filth. Ask her whether she would want the air-conditioned apartment in Forest Hills for her children. Ask her, then, whether she would be patient with someone who suggested that she and her children ought to "earn" a better standard of life when that is virtually impossible in the circumstances under which she and her children are forced to live.

When my argument is concluded I haven't convinced any of them, but I think they begin to feel less confident in their "No Project—No Way" stance. Their sense of practicality begins to creep in, and they are less sure that they are willing to gamble on an all-or-nothing-at-all basis. It's too early to be certain, but I feel strongly the repeated body blows through the first ten rounds are beginning to force their guard down, and this is good, because I'm convinced that the only answer here lies somewhere between the polar extremes of both groups. But even if I am right, this is only Scylla; there still remains to be dealt with a very large black Charybdis.

Friday, June 23, 1972

A retired sociologist who has taught both in Europe and this country and who lives in the Forest Hills area has talked to me several times about the situation. He knows and is respected by most of the principals. He called again today and we chatted awhile. He said that he thought Samuels' remarks earlier this week were unfortunate, but that in all candor he felt the entire opposition group from Forest Hills was so distrustful of Lindsay that it was difficult for them to believe that I could be objective, since Lindsay had appointed me. He is a strong believer in mix, notwithstanding the objection that even middle-income units become low-income by attrition. I told him that I felt a mix of middle and low was good, and that had the project been limited to a couple of hundred families the mix could have been accomplished by melding the two hundred families into the surrounding established community. At 840 units, however, the project is so large that it is in effect a separate community. Therefore, if left at that size, the mix must be accomplished internally. He agreed completely.

He said that Ed Smith,* formerly with the City Planning Department, wished to speak to me, so I fixed a date for 9:15 Monday night at Borough Hall.

Saturday, June 24, 1972

Miller was down from Boston. He had spent two years in the Department of City Planning working for the most part in the Staten Island office. He left to go back to MIT a couple of years ago. His father was a well-known apartment house builder, and his mother is at present a UDC housing economist. He was here for

* A pseudonym.

over four hours, and the following were some of the points he made.

1. He agreed that bringing in a large number of poor, and particularly welfare, would present a problem.

2. In 1966, at the genesis of the scatter-site program, the Lindsay administration had contracted with HUD to provide 7,500 units of low-income housing, and this, together with the political understanding that the borough president would have a veto vote, underlay the original program. Although people suspect that Sam Lefrak had a great deal to do with exchanging the project for a school in Corona, no one seems to know exactly how the selection of 108th Street came about. Lefrak probably would not have wanted the project, even at 108th Street.

3. There is no question that the Lindsay administration felt the "liberal" Jewish community of Forest Hills would be receptive to the project. They were wrong, but the judgment at the time was reasonable.

4. Miller reminded me that zoning was only fifty-six years old, and planning only about forty years old.

5. If Forest Hills does not get built, then the entire country may say "It won't work." By virtue of the federal requirement that we build in middle-income non-racially-concentrated areas, if projects are not built in places like Forest Hills, the result will be to dry up the supply of housing funds entirely. The public at large does not appear to be aware of this.

6. Compromise has to be intellectually honest and must be politically hard.

7. The biggest objection to any reduction will arise out of the necessity that the city contribute further monies to get fewer apartments. This would result from the fact that the project as presently designed is up to the federal per unit maximum contribution, and if you lower the number of units while keeping the basic costs—like land acquisition and curing—you will exceed HUD's maxima.

8. He would reduce to one fifteen-story tower and two fourteens, and would make up the difference in the money that the city would

have to pay for reducing the buildings by having other capital budget items that the city does not wish to move pulled out.

9. He reminded me that as originally conceived, the project—in Corona—would have had only 509 units to begin with.

(Upon any return to the Board of Estimate the issue would have to be framed in such a way that the only question to be reached would be the question of the alternative, leaving the original proposition intact if the resolution was turned down.)

Miller returned to Boston but said he would be available to talk to me—or even to come down again—any time I wished.

We went to Antun's tonight for the Piazza wedding, and Birbach, who is a good friend of the Piazza family, was at the same table. Although we got there very late, Jerry was still there and we were able to talk, on and off, for a couple of hours. Jerry sees himself as a great leader of limitless potential who has inspired the people of Forest Hills. And there's no doubt that to some extent he has. He made it crystal clear that his principal objection to compromise was that so far his people were not playing a "prominent" role in the process. Birbach showed great interest at the slightest hint from me that I would be willing to attribute any reasonable plan largely to him. He is both cute and bright, and his present game is very clearly simply to sit back and shoot down any suggestion that's made by me. Again, this is reminiscent of the Corona situation. He says he is very disturbed that so many of his residents have been in to see me, and he intends to disavow them as spokesmen for his group when the time comes. This is hardly consistent with his complaint that his people are not being consulted, but tactics in this kind of struggle need not be intelligent or consistent to be effective. The only compromise he would accept—according to him—is a garden apartment for the elderly. He talked about violence. He read somewhere that this country was born in violence, and he has produced out of that the nice generalization that violence can therefore be virtue. It comes as no surprise that he should be tempted by this extreme view—what else does he have left? If indeed he loses in the Court of Appeals, he has no argument to make—or, at least, no coercive device available. At that point the only muscle he can show, beyond the threat of massive exodus, is the threat of violence.

I repeatedly stated to Birbach that if I had to report at the present time, I would probably report that all compromise was out of the question because no compromise will suit the people of Forest Hills, and the city might therefore just as well go ahead with the 840 units as designed. He is uncomfortable with this suggestion, particularly since he suspects that I might lay the responsibility for the all-or-nothing-at-all approach at his door.

Jerry asked me a couple of times if I would call him, and I handled that very lightly. I told him I had already spoken to so many of his people that I didn't see any real point in having a "formal" discussion with him. Sooner or later he'll decide to call me and to make an appointment in the prescribed fashion. He can't afford to permit himself to be isolated.

With all that's happened and notwithstanding the charges Jerry has apparently flung at me, I can't really dislike him. I think in many ways he's being victimized by his own tactics. His people are apparently beyond his control. By taking the hard stance he did in the beginning, he set a tone and a theme which he can't now escape. Given his druthers, I think we'd be working something out right now.

Sunday, June 25, 1972

I spent all day today with the files. I read through everything in the materials I've accumulated, and prepared a new check list of areas to investigate. I'm probably as conversant now with the overall situation as anyone in town—and maybe more so. This coming week will have to be devoted to discussions of specifics with people like Congressmen Ed Koch and Ben Rosenthal, William Green of Housing and Urban Development, Chairman Don Elliot of the City Planning Commission, and Golar.

Monday, June 26, 1972

I reached Koch, Rosenthal, and Green on the phone. All of them are eager to talk, and I've made appointments—the latest one being

July 6, on which day we ought to have a decision from the Court of Appeals in the Forest Hills case.

Larry Marx* was at Borough Hall tonight with a neighbor. Marx is a ladies' lingerie manufacturer in the city and lives some thirteen blocks from the project in a rent-controlled apartment, as does his neighbor. Marx took an extremely hard stance. He was very clearly intending to rebut any notion I had that I was in any way reaching the Forest Hills residents. He told me that the reports of our meetings had been grim. Some people said that I was a total phony because I had called my own Corona people "stupid winos." Others had said that I have nothing but contempt for the Jewish community and said that they were "gutless." Two other gentlemen reported, according to Marx, that I had said, "All other projects in the city were vastly successful." Although I regard myself as fairly well-insulated against this kind of charge, these both surprised and stung me. Ben Liebman, a young student who is doing research for a paper and who has been present on several occasions at my meetings, said that he was aghast at the reports from Marx. He remembered references to wine, references to other projects, and references to Jewish resiliency that I had made, but if Marx was telling the truth they were all dramatically distorted by the Forest Hills people.

There are at least two possibilities: the Forest Hills residents are so hung-up emotionally that they interpret any hint at disagreement with their position as a mark that the speaker is an enemy. They then proceed to do what you do to enemies—which is to cast them in the worst possible light so as to keep the adrenaline flowing high. The other possibility is that Marx and Birbach are simply trying to play what may be their last card. I earlier noted Birbach's comments on Saturday about the threat of violence. Having thought about that over the weekend, he may very well have agreed and told Marx to take a strong "violence" position with me. That would have to start by making it clear that there was no real chance for a compromise.

Marx, a businessman, and presumably reasonable, refused to

* A pseudonym.

consider any alternative other than garden apartments for the elderly. I'm sure that in business he would have taken a more flexible position. I didn't try very hard to argue against the violence theme; it seemed to me so obviously wrong that I didn't think there was much point in elaborating. Besides, I'm sure they're not serious about it.

Following Marx were Ed Smith, formerly of the Department of City Planning, and my sociologist friend from Forest Hills. Smith says 108th Street was selected by a committee consisting of Elliot, Ed Robin and Eugenia Flatow. It is his opinion that the site was selected in a great hurry and was attractive mostly because it was vacant. There was no real study made, according to him.

Smith felt that the Forest Hills community is, in effect, on the brink of decay; many of the apartment houses are old and could "turn around" very easily. He suggested that the UDC come in and take the project over in its entirety and use its 70–20–10 formula. I told him I had been trying to reach the governor's counsel in order to discuss that possibility but that I had no luck in getting through. (I can't blame the governor's office for not being eager to get involved.) He suggested an interesting tenant-selection process which would consist of taking the cream of the tenants from other projects and placing them in Forest Hills—or any other new low-income project. This could be rationalized as providing incentives for people to live well in projects. It would, in effect, make of the older projects a kind of "European halfway house." I'll try it out on some of the black leaders.

On the matter of 236 spin-off, he pointed out it would be better to mix internally within the same building. He acknowledged that left at twenty-four stories most of the Forest Hills residents would regard the mix as simply a temporary condition and that eventually it would become fully low-income.

A thought crossed my mind while listening to him. Some of his suggestions were good. But for some reason—perhaps it was accumulated fatigue—I was struck with the massive complexity of trying to work out a solution and the real possibility that whatever was worked out would be vigorously rejected by everyone. It occurred to me that conceivably the whole idea of discussing compromise might prove to have been a mistake. Maybe it would have been better simply to leave it to the Court of Appeals and to let the project take its course, instead of, perhaps, adding fuel to the fire by permitting the Forest Hills community another opportunity to make its case. That was my first thought. I recovered somewhat. My second was that there is still a chance that a solution can be arrived at which the majority, so far silent, will recognize as reasonable, and which will be sufficiently attractive to inspire them into affecting public opinion and, therefore, the political palatability of the solution.

As an insider, Smith was able to give me a good feel for what actually happened here. From the beginning it has been a series of mistakes and miscalculations. The very idea of scatter-site was, to start with, virtually untested—almost purely a social experiment—and the attempt to move on it massively in several different locations appears now, in retrospect, to have been a great error, no matter how noble the intentions. This is worse when one considers that in all likelihood the reason it needed to be done this way was that the only way to get it past the borough presidents was to make each borough president suffer equally, and also that the federal government had created arbitrary requirements with respect to the number of units that had to be built citywide. Beginning with a dubious concept, the chances for success were further minimized by selecting a site in a less than careful manner. The last-minute switch in Corona, even if totally honorable, was bound to produce cynical reaction because of the failure of explanation. The lack of machinery for community consultation exacerbated the problem even more. Anyone who has experienced the process knows that there was no real vehicle, particularly six years ago, for community input. The local planning boards were just then beginning to function, and they were largely disregarded, as was the case in Forest Hills. I have always regarded the hearings at the Planning Commission and Board of Estimate as an unfortunate and sometimes cruel joke. As Forest Hills—and Corona, Glen Oaks,*

---

* The Glen Oaks and Parkway Village situations in Queens involved city approvals to permit high-rise construction.

and Parkway Village—have shown, the hearing system is so transparently a ploy that it often has the effect of further antagonizing the community groups. It's one thing to abuse people; it's another to do it flagrantly and hypocritically. Communities have achieved enough sophistication so that now they have to be treated with some respect for their intelligence. It's not enough to provide them with a stage. The early hearings in the Forest Hills situation were nothing more. And the matter of the HUD guidelines, which were vague, inconstant, and were eventually altered. Then the extended period of inactivity that followed the site selection created an opportunity for people to be lulled into a false sense that no project would be built. They relaxed their guard and, as a result, lost the opportunity to solve both the Corona and 108th Street problems by moving the school to 108th Street.

Now, finally, we arrive at a stage where most people agree that Forest Hills was a mistake—at least in terms of its size. Can it be that given this history of miscalculation, there is no way of undoing it or at least mitigating it?

Smith pointed out that a building totally for the elderly may be vulnerable, as is the Stanton Street Project in Manhattan. Deviants of all types apparently feel they have an easy mark when the building is completely for the elderly.

The sociologist repeated his ideas about mix, and made it clear that he is disturbed by my apparent opinion that perhaps no compromise at all is feasible. He wants to be sure that I do not overreact to the Forest Hills Residents Association position and he insists that there is a silent majority that will speak up when the time comes. It's working.

I spoke to Tom McMahon late tonight. I played ball with him years ago in South Jamaica, and he's now a detective in the district attorney's office. Tom was brought up in projects and he's had a lot of familiarity with them throughout the city as a policeman. He says they are all "murder." He thinks the city is foolish for even considering 840 units in Forest Hills. If he were commissioner he would assign a special task force to the area if the project must be built.

Hector Knowles,* director of an urban renewal program in Nassau, called me today. He is black and very knowledgeable in the housing field. He's traveled all over the country, and says that he regards the Forest Hills project as "disgraceful"—840 units are much too much. He believes in the elderly/middle-income/low-income mix. I said that I felt Wilkins' integration position was not necessarily referable to low-income housing; it was equally compatible with middle-income housing. He agreed. He said most blacks would disagree with the Forest Hills project and those he has spoken with have done so. Some blacks even feel that the way the project is designed might even be a deliberate attempt to isolate them. Knowles says the only way to have upward mobility is to put upper-strata people in the same building, i.e., middle-income. He doesn't want to be quoted because he's afraid it would put him at odds with some of the black leaders.

I spoke to Eddie Effros, attorney for P. J. Carlin, the contractor at the site. He said the city can have the contract if it wants it. All it has to do is buy it. Effros is making it clear he will give nothing away. He also made it clear he would be willing to talk with the mayor to discuss changes in the contract if that was necessary to achieve a compromise.

I spent the evening reading—among other materials—Roger Starr's *Commentary* article and the *Village Voice* treatment of the Twin Parks Project, which has erupted into a conflict between the Italians, blacks, and Puerto Ricans.

Wednesday, June 28, 1972

I spent only an hour with William Green of HUD today, but it was productive. Green is a bright lawyer—Harvard-trained—pleasant enough, and, apparently, frank. There is no doubt in my mind that he regards the project as a small fiasco, although he never so stated. He was careful to point out that he was not here when the project was originally selected. He also notes that had the present HUD project criteria been applicable in 1966, this project might not have

* A pseudonym.

qualified. He pointed particularly to the criterion which requires that the project be "buildable promptly." Green suggests this project would not have passed that test.

He points out that there is a newly proposed housing bill—and this is extremely important—since it may permit HUD to use an administrative level for 236 money which will free a great deal of additional funds for the city. The bill is now in the House Banking and Currency Committee, and both Koch and Congressman Frank Brasco are on that committee.

We had a good talk about Section 23 leasing of apartments for low-income tenants in existent private apartment houses. Green likes the idea. He said that if we could find 600 to under 1,000 units, he could finance it in the 1973 allocation. He thought the problems were the legal limit on rent, which is about $200, and the reluctance of private apartment house owners in good areas to "risk" their investments by moving even a few low-income people in. He regards this approach as an excellent one if it can be worked out and would be delighted to help. He will get me specifics on the legal limits.

At my request, Green will give me figures on the cost of cutting down—all the way to twelve stories. He suggested that it might be easier simply to eliminate a tower altogether and will give me figures on that as well. He also wondered about replacing one of the towers with a mini-school.

I asked Green whether it was possible to buy back the whole deal, and he said that he thought we could buy him out for the amount of money expended by the federal government to date— which is approximately $8 million. This curious possibility arose— and I put it to Green: conceivably it would be cheaper to buy back the federal investment, and then to go back to the board with a packaged proposition that says, "Kill the project as is, on condition that it be replaced with a new one." Green will give me figures on that possibility.

Green thinks that in the new allocation he may be able to come up with 236 money for us—if the new law goes through. He did not react badly to my suggestion that perhaps all three buildings could go 236, with an agreement that 40 percent (the legal maximum) go for low income: that would be about 336 low-income and 504 middle.

He thought that redesigning the project so that it would be totally for the elderly would be extremely expensive, and he will have his experts look at this, too.

Green felt the principal environmental impact would be with high schools but that the new high school in Corona would alleviate that problem substantially.

With respect to cooperatives, he thought the guidelines at present might not permit cooperatives in a new high rise where straight low-income elderly and families would make up the population. He suggested I check this out further with some of his staff.

Thursday, June 29, 1972

Reverend Joseph H. May of the Baptist Ministers Conference was here for nearly two hours this morning. He has a church in the Rockaways. He's sixtyish with a beautiful soft face and manner but tall and straight and firm. I can't imagine that anyone could have made the case for the low-income people any better. An extremely sensitive individual, a man of intelligence and restraint but still powerfully moved not only by a brooding emotional commitment to his people but near (as near as a good minister will let himself get) resentment for the nonblack forces in society that have suppressed and oppressed his people. May sees the issue very simply: the project will provide good homes and living conditions for poor people, many of whom are black; it is wrong morally to deprive them of even a single unit; it is particularly wrong to do so after the governmental process has operated. Reverend May does not spend a great deal of thought on the question as to how projects have affected other areas; the issue is to him an almost purely moral and philosophical one. He will concede that the middle class is moving out of the city but attributes that responsibility to them, exclusively. He regards the present struggle as one between the Jews and the blacks and feels that a victory for them would be another evidence of their political strength born of money and education. When I pointed out that many of the opponents felt that the decision to build in Forest Hills was actually the result of "black" political strength, May became indignant.

What a sad situation that no one will even consider the possibility that the judgment, wise or not, was a matter of principle and not politics. Was it ever thus? Can it change?

It was clear that May's objection to "compromise" was heightened by the fear that any return to the Board of Estimate for a so-called compromise would actually result in killing the project entirely. I told him that I thought that could be obviated legally but he wasn't sure he could believe me.

He did not like the "cream" theory of selecting tenants from other projects. He felt it was demeaning to his people. "Why should they have to prove themselves?" On the other hand, he agreed that any court decision which might prevent removal of a tenant from a project, although the tenant was proven to be "undesirable," would be a bad rule. He would say so publicly.

After he made his case, I argued the other side. He softened somewhat, but under no circumstances could he accept cutting the project down to fewer than 600 tenant units.

He would not approve of increasing the number of elderly or a mix. The greater need is with the low-income families.

Whom does May speak for? Not Eddie, who works in the barbershop downstairs. He is black and has two children. He's a vet. He's been to Europe and Korea. He spent an even tougher tour growing up in Harlem for ten years. He doesn't want to live in a project or near one because he feels the low-income and welfare elements are destructive and troublesome. He knows their problem and he sympathizes with them, but why spread the problem? He does not see the issue as a "black" issue; he sees it as an issue of "working people" and nonworking people. He does not think leaders who live in Jamaica Estates and Scarsdale represent him.

Eddie shook my hand today and thanked me for trying to "help out with a hard problem." He believes we're trying to do something right. I have the strong feeling that most of those who have been in to see me aren't ready to accept that. They start with the assumption that no one would get involved in this mess without some venal if not downright crooked reason. No one knows for sure, but many of them imagine that this is all a rigged device to get Lindsay off the hook or to fool the community into relenting in their opposition for a while so that the building can be built and the matter put beyond their reach. They're tentative, suspicious, cautious. Most of them feel the way Samuels does but don't express it as clearly as he did to me. Many of them, on both sides, have checked around the city trying to figure out what the "game" is. I know because I get calls almost every day from various friends— some in the Jewish and black organizations, some in government— telling me that people have been asking around about me. I can't blame them for their suspicions; I'd probably feel the same way they do. This is particularly true because every night as we sit through these meetings I argue both sides of the case. That has an unsettling effect on many of them; no one is less to be trusted than a man without a position. But with it all, they are coming in and we are getting a reliable expression of all views. In that respect, this entire process is probably unique. I doubt there has ever been a situation where such a full opportunity to be heard on a local issue has been afforded. That, by itself, will be a positive good. But we'll have to accomplish much more to make this excruciating effort worthwhile.

Tonight I was at Borough Hall for a meeting with the Eastern Queens Synagogues. Manes called me in the afternoon to say he was meeting with the Lashinsky–Samuels group tonight and he didn't want me to be "upset" by it. Tonight some of them (neither Lashinsky nor Samuels was included) came from their meeting with Manes. They fear I have already "sold out" and they're trying to protect themselves by keeping the heat on Manes. Birbach is doing the same thing; he picketed Manes' house today and made a public statement that he has still not heard from Cuomo (which he insists on pronouncing "Que-mo"). Would you believe? I told the group I thought their game-playing was counter-productive, but I talked to them anyway for over an hour. There was nothing new in their arguments or their positions on compromise. Krim, one of their attorneys, would recommend a mix and warned me about overstating their reluctance to compromise. A reasonable man, but probably too frank for their taste. They are great bargainers; they feel they should maintain the hardest possible stance. "No project, no way"—or at most, garden apartments for the elderly.

An early night—home by 11:30.

Friday, June 30, 1972

The sociologist called to report that the Queens Jewish Community Council had been to Washington and had been told by some Congressman that I had already committed myself to a compromise that would leave the buildings as they are now planned. They were angry about it. Would that they were right! It would certainly save me a lot of trouble. I'm convinced there is no point in straining to assure everyone that we're telling the truth. It would only make matters worse.

I spoke with Congressman Joe Addabbo on the phone. He said the Rochdale Project in his area in Queens was a mess with a serious crime problem, so serious that they have their own auxiliary police. He says the project at Forest Hills must be scaled down. He liked the idea of two towers and a mini-school. I stressed it would have to be an intermediate school because the high school would be built in Corona. Addabbo also thought we should consider some sort of multipurpose building with federal funds.

Saturday, July 1, 1972

My good friend Bob Sharkey from Horn came through for me. He's found out that although piling for the entire complex will not be completed until September, they will be capping piles by July 15 and may get up into the air with superstructure on one of the buildings by August 15. I had better turn my report in before the buildings are built.

Wednesday, July 5, 1972

The return of the infection in my jaw has made it difficult to do much for the last few days; the antibiotics have kept me semistupefied. I would have it taken care of except that it would probably cost me ten days or so, which I can ill afford now.

I was able to reread, very carefully, the final Environmental Statement prepared by HUD with comments and responses. If I had this document with its exhibits a few weeks ago it would have made this problem much easier. It's an excellent treatment of everything but the purely sociological, political, and legal arguments.

In today's mail I received a lengthy commentary from Ben Liebman, the student who has sat through some hearings with me. There's nothing new or exciting in it but it confirms my view on many of the points he treats.

Stanley Lane, a Jewish Republican Conservative leader from Hollis Hills called. He and I went to Shimer Junior High School together twenty-eight years ago. His parents live in Forest Hills, and he wanted to go on record in opposition to the project. He started by telling me how far-ranging are the rumors concerning me personally: I am involved in the compromise just to bail out Gold; I have no intention of listening to the Forest Hills people; I have not really spent any time in the community and I am generally no good. This was by way of prefacing his solution which would get me off the hook and into the good graces of the Forest Hills community. His plan—kill the project before it kills Forest Hills. Put in its place two office buildings—one city, one state—and a municipal parking garage. That certainly would make me a hero in Forest Hills!

Don Manes also called to say he thought I would be blasted by Samuels and Lashinsky for "inaction."

I must admit, if only to myself, that the criticism is annoying. No decision yet from the Court of Appeals. Tomorrow's the day.

Thursday, July 6, 1972

About ten days ago I had met with Joe DeVoy, Mike Dowd, and Marino Jeantet—all local Community Board chairmen in the affected area. All three indicated they think there should be some compromise and will treat almost any reduction in size as a victory.

Obviously they each have their own ideas as to what the best compromise would be, but I think that regardless of the details, they will be helpful about any reasonable attempt to make the project more workable.

This morning I met with Congressman Koch and two of his aides. He told me that some months ago he, Rosenthal, Matt Troy,* and Manes had discussed and agreed upon a compromise which consisted of cutting all three buildings down and then making up the lost units in other parts of Queens.

We talked about the effect of Forest Hills on the future of the scatter-site housing program nationwide. A major part of the problem is created by the vagueness of the terminology. If scatter site is taken to mean the building of projects that are exclusively or largely low-income in middle-income areas, then I'm not sure that it is a workable concept. It has no real history and there is no firm basis on which to conclude that it will work. On the other hand, if scatter site is taken to mean the dispersal of public assistance so as to permit low-income people to live in nonracially restricted areas, then it is no longer a question of workability but rather a matter of law. The point is that the law can be complied with without building projects. Thus, Section 23 leasing might be a more effective device, as would be 236 mix buildings. In short, one can subscribe to the proposition that the poor should be permitted to live free from the tawdry and debasing influence of the ghetto, but that does not require a commitment to institutional living. Koch seemed to agree and was particularly pleased with the Section 23 idea.

Koch appears to be a little self-conscious about his position on the issue; it has apparently embarrassed him with many liberals. He feels that Wilkins does not truly speak for the blacks when he takes a strong position in favor of the project as is. He says he has spoken to many black individuals, some of them political leaders, and they have all indicated to him their disagreement with the present scale of the project. However, Koch points out that none of

* Matthew Troy, Democratic county leader of Queens County and a city councilman.

these people would dare make this statement publicly. I've had the same reaction.

I also spoke with Percy Sutton,* and he said he would be glad to talk to me when he gets back from the Democratic Convention in Miami.

Frank Krupp called. He had some interesting things to say about crime statistics and promised to put it all in a note to me.

The constant theme from all the opponents of the project: "Why don't they spend the money in the bombed-out areas? Why jeopardize the sound middle-income area when half of East New York has been left in rubble?" The theme is simple enough and as a matter of fact has apparently been the housing policy of the nation until recently. The idea of scatter site is new. The argument overlooks a number of things:

1. The conclusion by many that upward mobility can best be generated by moving poor people out of the stultifying, degrading environment of the ghetto (that was the Koerner Commission's conclusion);

2. The law: there is simply no legal choice. As a matter of constitutional law the city could not spend its federal housing funds exclusively in ghetto areas. Perhaps the federal law is not wise, but for the time being one must live with it;

3. The fact that we *are* continuing to build in bombed-out areas. Scatter site is only an adjunct to that program and, relatively, a very small adjunct.

Friday, July 7, 1972

I met with Police Commissioner Patrick Murphy and his special counsel this morning. Murphy agreed that crime and poverty are obviously associated and that any concentration of low-income tenants—and, particularly, welfare people—in an area may well have the effect of increasing the crime rate. He has no statistics to prove this, but he feels that it would be commonly accepted. While he did not say so directly, he left me with the impression that

---

* Borough president of New York County.

statistics as to crime within projects are not necessarily indicative of the overall situation. He described the effect as a "stone in a pond; the waves go out from the center."

The commissioner was not clear on the relationship between crime and the scale of buildings, although he knew that Dr. Newman and others were studying it.

We had an interesting discussion on tenant selection. The commissioner's counsel strongly defended the refusal on the basis of civil rights to turn over arrest records. He was quite persuasive but was willing, as was the commissioner, to discuss the matter with Housing Authority officials. I should make a point of bringing this to Golar's attention.

The only suggestion the commissioner had with respect to the Police Department's assistance with the new project was to contact the crime prevention officer in the 112th Precinct in Forest Hills and possibly the citywide commanding officer in charge of crime prevention. Captain Leibman of the 112th Precinct is the man to talk to, and I will.

I have not read any of the stories in today's paper about the "scene" outside of Jeantet's Restaurant during the Corona victory celebration last night, but I have been peppered with reports all day. The *Times*, I'm told, reported that Birbach called me a fraud. Jerry telephoned me this afternoon to say that he had been misquoted—he claims he said the mayor was a fraud and not me. I told him it didn't make any difference and that I would make no public comment on it. I also told him I thought some of his people behaved like animals and he said they were "upset."

There was literally a near riot caused by their attempts to storm the mayor, who was celebrating with the ecstatically happy Corona people last night. At one point there were about a hundred and fifty Forest Hills residents outside the restaurant chanting and screaming. Thirty or so policemen had them under control, but the fuse was burning. One of the officers in charge asked me to talk to the group and I went out on the street with them. There was a lot of pushing and shoving and some stupid kid—for no reason—leaned over a circle of people surrounding me and slapped me in the face. I grabbed for him but was stopped. I'm glad I was; I'm not sure what I might have done at that instant. In the melee Lilly Manasseri, who was there with the residents, was knocked down and injured. She was crying like a baby and I helped her into the ambulance after trying to calm her down by chatting with her for a few minutes. She was totally helpless, but the ambulance attendant thought she'd be all right. I expect she'll be back in Forest Hills in a few days telling everybody how I "sold her out" in Corona.

The media called all day for comments on the Court of Appeals' decision today affirming the Appellate Division 6–1 with Judge Scileppi dissenting. I was out of the office most of the day and missed them—it's probably just as well. Now Birbach has lost the election and the residents have lost their suit. Will it affect their position?

Saturday, July 8, 1972

I spoke with Judy Goldman this morning, and as usual she was perceptive and cogent. She made some points, among which were the following (with some elaboration by me):

1. It's ironic that people should now regard the Jews of Forest Hills as bigots when in fact it's known that Jews have traditionally led the way in civil rights causes. What of the Jewish boys who gave their lives in Mississippi? The Jews are not opposed to the color of the potential tenants; they're opposed to the deterioration that is threatened by the intrusion of large numbers of low-income people.

2. There is such a strongly fixed prejudice against Jews by blacks generally, i.e., the notion that Jews are exploiters, that there is no point in trying to change the impression. Thus one ought not to be concerned about whether the report will exacerbate black hostility with the Jews as a class.

3. Should the moral obligation require the Forest Hills people to embrace their low-income brethren even at the risk of deterioration? Yes, if it can be said that the project is good for its potential tenants, and so the question becomes: Is it good? And the answer is "yes" if the Forest Hills residents can supply for their brethren an "upward mobility." Then the question becomes: Will the proximity supply this kind of example and inspiration? And to this, there is

no clear answer. On the one hand is the possible psychological problem of a confrontation between the haves and have-nots. Commissioner Murphy noted this as a problem. Frank Krupp points out that judged from his experience, the Forest Hills area would undoubtedly be particularly vulnerable to the kind of crime that would be generated by large numbers of low-income people. The predetermined "example" may be the example that they provide for one another, instead of the example that the external community provides for each of them.

4. We seem to have a history in this city of deteriorating sound institutions in an attempt to uplift the "lower" elements. Surely this has happened with the school system, and the Jews have been particularly affected by this, since they are such strong users of the public institutions. The threat as they now see it is that we will drag down another area of strength in our city—to wit, the middle-class communities. Logically projected, the eventual deterioration of all middle-class communities will make the city one sprawling ghetto, and thus the question becomes: What is the greater good: the breaking up of the ghettos at the risk of deteriorating middle-income areas or the insulation of the middle-income areas at the risk of exacerbating the cycle of poverty? It would be easy to conclude that these hard questions are unanswerable but we can't afford that luxury. Some attempt at reconciling these forces *must* be made.

5. Perhaps the real bigotry is with the so-called liberal who demonstrates a remarkable inability to appreciate any part of the arguments made by the "middle class."

6. The impression remains strong that projects have been built mainly in Jewish areas.

7. To cut the project in half is merely to leave both sides totally unsatisfied. To leave the project intact would disturb the opponents. There is no satisfactory answer.

It occurred to me today that the report should mention the impact of the political considerations. There is no way of winning political points with a compromise, and this administration and the Board of Estimate will recognize this. The only question here should be: What is the best course for the city at large regardless of what the immediate reaction will be? It seems clear to me at this point that the best course is somewhere in the middle, notwithstanding the fact that it would be the most dangerous course politically, since it will result in leaving both sides antagonized instead of just one. The antagonism may pass, given the fickleness of people's political judgments; the housing crisis, the problem of a threatened stability of middle-class areas, and the threat to the housing program itself will not pass, and they are the areas of concern that should be decisive.

This project was an experiment and should have been treated as such. There is a threat. The threat should have been reduced by making the project as small as possible. This is not unfair to the project population because the scale hurts even them. To the extent that it is swollen and becomes an enclave, it reduces the chance for upward mobility, so that even the project tenants themselves should want it to be smaller. Scatter-siting should be accomplished by continuing to build in slum clearance projects, rehabilitating old communities, Section 23 leasing, small mix units, and home ownership devices like the cooperatives.

It is entirely possible that this whole problem will be treated in an entirely different way in the near future. Even George Romney concedes that the housing program overall has been a fiasco and that a new approach is needed. But that will take time; in the meanwhile some steps must be taken, and this is only a very small one.

Monday, July 10, 1972

The string is fast running out; the report must be filed within two weeks. Under the circumstances it's plainly impossible to do the job that this problem deserves. But with the contractor about to get into the air on his first building, I have no choice but to sum up. Even assuming I had already formulated a reasonably clear plan, the actual writing of the report would have presented a problem. In fact, there is no plan yet. I don't even have the necessary figures from HUD, and without them no plan can be formulated. I met with Leo Haberman and Arthur Brenner of HUD this morning, and they expect to have the figures for me by Wednesday.

It will also be impossible to gather opinions and support regarding my suggestions before they are published, thereby further complicating an already complex situation. It seems now that the report will be filed without my knowing what degree of acceptance it's likely to have. This presents a very real possibility that the report will be universally rejected and the entire effort will prove to have been a huge waste. All of this is disturbing; all of it is made worse by the increase of personal abuse. Being slapped by a young nut outside of Jeantet's last week was nearly enough to produce an explosion. What is tougher is the lousy phone calls I've been receiving in increasing numbers both at home and in the office. Abuse by anonymous offenders is hard to take.

In any event, both Haberman and Brenner of HUD had given this matter a good deal of thought. While they are vague on the numbers, they make clear their conclusion that a reduction of anything more than four floors in each tower would be a "horrible expense." Haberman's thought was to reduce all towers to 20, make one a 236 and one a Mitchell-Lama. They made the following points among others:

1. The center building has the central heating plant, and if one whole tower were to be eliminated, it would have to be one of the end towers. At that, the heating plant will be overdesigned.

2. If the building is reduced enough, you might avoid the drainage problem, i.e., the pumping station. They had no figures on this.

3. Similarly, if one building were taken out, you would save the pumping facilities for that building.

Haskell Lazere also called asking what I had done to Samuels and Co. He was referring to the strong position I had taken with the QJCC concerning their unilateral participation. I told him what had happened. To some extent like Birbach, the QJCC is seeking to maintain their identity by not being absorbed into this "compro-

mise" process. I did learn, however, that my repeated mention of
the hard stance being taken by the Forest Hills residents has had
the effect hoped for. Lazere tells me he has seen evidence of some
"breakthroughs."

Jerry called me at home. He was affable, and indicated concern
over my frequent trips to the doctor. Apparently someone had told
him about the problem I was having and he pressed me for details.
Jerry's reason for calling was simply to ask whether he could come
to talk to me with one or two of his board members. I told him that
I had never refused to talk to any of his people and I would
certainly not exclude him. Jerry would like to make it a luncheon
meeting, probably to avoid having to come to my office or to
Borough Hall.

Now, consider what's happened:

Birbach started six weeks ago talking to me privately but
publicly demanding to speak directly and exclusively with the
mayor. He dropped back from that position to the concession that
he would talk to both the mayor and Cuomo together. When I said
that I would refuse to meet under those circumstances he agreed
that if I would formally and publicly request an interview I would
be permitted to come to the Forest Hills Residents' meeting. When
I explained that I preferred my approach of seeking out no one but
accepting all requests, he hung back. Now, finally, rather than
isolate himself entirely he's come forward on the same basis as all
the others who wished to participate. It's hopeful. It seems now that
the original thought, which was to involve Birbach in this process,
but only on a basis that would not make it appear that he was a
determinant, has worked. This could be extremely important.
Obviously, one of the basic justifications for any compromise
would be to keep the Forest Hills community intact and to avoid
the kind of heated discontent which would both endanger the
project and threaten exodus. A mollified, or at least reasonable,
Birbach can help assure that result, although it could conceivably
be accomplished without him. I told Jerry I'd call him back
tomorrow morning.

Tuesday, July 11, 1972

Lieberman was in this morning. He's a math teacher (between jobs at the moment), who has devoted a good deal of time to the Forest Hills situation. His five-page paper was carefully thought out. It starts with a suggestion that the Corona High School be moved to 108th Street and ends with a recommendation that "rehabilitation camps" be built on the outskirts of the city. In between, Lieberman touches on the idea of Section 23 dispersal.

Lieberman described for me some of the things I've been accused of by the Birbach group (the "ignorant winos" distortion, etc.). He's convinced now that these things were not true, and that's a matter of some small satisfaction.

Lieberman made an interesting comment. He said, in a somewhat loose reference to the biblical passage, that Forest Hills is now reaping what we, as a nation, sowed two hundred and fifty years ago. We brought the slaves and then left them to survive without our assistance, and indeed, against our resistance. The result is that many of them have grown to be weeds now threatening to choke the "garden" of Forest Hills. I'm not sure many of his neighbors would appreciate his philosophical rationalization for their present woes.

I also spoke to Patrolman Motto at the 112th Precinct. He's the crime prevention officer and takes his job very seriously. There's every reason to believe that as soon as the project begins accepting tenants—and even before then—he will be able to run an effective survey and education program which will both anticipate problems and be helpful in preventing or mitigating them. He pointed out there is a special youth patrolman—DeMuro—who has an extensive program now running. He will have DeMuro call me.

Wednesday, July 12, 1972

We've had more success than I expected with the strongest opponents. I got word today that Seymour Samuels wants to come in again. He, like Birbach, has apparently concluded that it would be wiser for them to participate in this process than to stand aloof.

The time for fact gathering is over; now's the time for analysis. More than fifteen years of dealing with complicated factual situations is going to help. I started last night going through all of the materials again and breaking them down into points. I'll have them on cards by Friday night, and by Monday I should be able to start dictating; there won't be time to write.

Things are happening very rapidly now. The HUD people are working frantically to get me the figures I need and I talk to them a couple of times a day. Commissioner Nat Leventhal of the Housing and Development Administration gave me a couple of hours Friday morning. I needed to talk to him concerning the possibility of a Mitchell-Lama.

Now conclusions begin to suggest themselves. In order to satisfy any substantial number of opponents, there will need to be either a substantial cut in the size of the project, say 50 percent, or a lesser scaling down with a change in the mix. If the bottom four floors were to be removed, that would take out most of the large bedroom units, with the result that there would be fewer children and probably more elderly. I'm waiting for the exact number from HUD. I'm convinced that a reduction to 18, with one building going for Mitchell-Lama, would not be enough from the Forest Hills side. But is it not also too much for the other side to take? That would leave you with approximately 420 low-income units and 210 Mitchell-Lama units. Of the 420 proposed, 200 units would be elderly, leaving only 220 family units. How would this be justified to the proponents? Say:

1. Scatter site is experimental.

2. Housing programs have generally had a dubious history and have an even more dubious future.

3. The closest comparable successful project is Latimer Gardens and that's 423 low-income units.

4. The *Gautreaux* case said that three-story 240 units was scatter-site.

5. The congestion problem, the scale problem.

6. The threat to the housing program generally.

7. The fact that the large size is apt simply to create a new ghetto.

8. The resentment factor.

9. The availability of other programs, e.g., Section 23, rehabilitation, etc.

10. And be careful with this: the fact that a sizable number of blacks—e.g., Baisley Park in Queens, Town of North Hempstead—have themselves indicated a disagreement with huge projects.

11. The symbolic aspect of the project is intact.

12. And here's a very tricky one: if the low-income sector has a vested right in 840 units, it is because government gave it to them. They themselves have conceded that if government were to operate again through the Board of Estimate, they would probably lose all 840 units. The proponents would say that if that judgment were to be made by government, it would be a bigoted one and therefore invalid. The Forest Hills people can say with equal cogency that the earlier governmental determination was itself vulnerable and the product of obverse bigotry. Why should not the people of Forest Hills have the same right to a governmental decision now that the proponents of the project had five years ago?

I spoke with Congressman Ben Rosenthal and told him I was waiting for the HUD figures. Rosenthal says that he regards large projects as "poverty incestuousness" and "warehouse" housing.

Ben agreed with me that Forest Hills may very well be the last large housing project in the city. He says the direction of the law has been away from this sort of housing. Section 23 dispersal is a lot more attractive to him, as it is to me.

We also agree that regionalization is part of the answer and that an all-out effort should be made to force the suburbs to scatter-site, just as we. This can be done administratively through HUD and, if necessary, by a proliferation of lawsuits. Ben actually feels that regionalization is the answer not only to housing but to education and many other problems. Obviously, it's not the whole answer but it's part of the formula.

I tried on Rosenthal my point on the right to a governmental judgment, and he agreed that while it was intellectually sound, it was nonsalable.

Ben would like to hear an outline of my report before it gets published and I promised I'd get back to him.

He is one of the few politicians who have taken a public stance on this issue from the beginning notwithstanding the obvious perils. If I didn't know him so well I probably would be surprised, but the fact is, he's never been anything but upright and honest in his work. He's one of the exceptional politicians who have not lost their integrity—that will probably cost him dearly in his political career. Integrity appears to be something of a rare commodity in politics, and when present it's normally a burden.

John Simon of the Housing Authority called and gave this information with respect to Latimer Gardens in Flushing—the low-income housing project nearest to the site:

—423 units;
—35 percent of the apartments are studio or one-bedroom;
—141 units are elderly;
—The overall percentage of blacks is 31 percent.
—There are 325 children out of a total population of 985;
—2.4 is the average family size;
—The buildings are 10 stories high.

Simon was pleased about my discussion with Commissioner Murphy. His feeling is that if H.A. can get records as to arrests and convictions it will be a "tremendous" help in tenant selection. He said he would tell Golar about my conversation and particularly my point that the commissioner's counsel's civil rights argument assumed an abuse by the H.A. that was neither proven nor fairly to be anticipated.

Simon also liked the simple suggestion I made that lights be supplied for the outdoor basketball courts and said he will do something about it. Can you think of a better way of keeping kids out of trouble in the hot summer months than playing basketball until midnight on a good court?

I mentioned the possibility of calling the development anything but Forest Hills. "Rego Gardens" rang a bell with him.

HUD has been extremely cooperative. They talked to me several times today and got me the figures at five o'clock tonight. A quick look tells me they are very complicated, and I decided to put them away until I could get a fresh look tomorrow morning.

Haskell Lazere and Seymour Sammit of the American Jewish Committee were in late this afternoon. A good talk with good people. They've spent a great deal of time and effort putting together a program designed to bring to bear all possible services and forces to make workable whatever project is built. The description they gave me today was impressive. I'll have it in my hands in written form by Friday morning.

I met with Birbach, Marty Wunderman, and then later in the night Howard Margulis, of the F.H.R.A. We had dinner at Jeantet's. I could not help being struck by the irony of the situation. A week ago Birbach had led his troopers in an assault on the restaurant during the Corona party and was publicly quoted as having called me a "fraud" and a "political ploy." Here, a week later, at his request and with the utmost affability, he was having dinner with me.

The conversation went quickly from the casual to the substantial. Birbach announced with all the firmness he could muster that unless the project is changed so that it will be "livable" in his opinion, he would publicly place his house for sale to a black, and would lead a massive emigration from Forest Hills, tearing down in his wake the whole community. He would, said Birbach, "burn down the town" rather than let the project tenants destroy it. While he made some passing references to violence, he later said that he agreed with my comments on the subject (made a couple of weeks ago) and that he would eschew any real violent conduct. Wunderman was silent through this part of Birbach's presentation. The approach had been plotted out carefully. Birbach was going to start by coming on strong. This was no surprise; to Jerry, subtlety is weakness. Before even talking about any change in the project I was very clear in telling Jerry that I regarded his position as wrong. I said that I could not see what his approach would accomplish and that it was nothing but a plan of retribution. I also told him that I doubted he meant what he said. In my own judgment, his pride and intelligence would not permit him to leave the scene. I suggested to him that a more intelligent approach for him to take would be to announce that the proposed compromise (whatever it is) was a sham and that his people had been "taken." He then could add that he would not be chased from the scene and would instead stand and fight to protect the investments of his people by making the most of the situation. "I am your leader and I will not desert you now that you need me more than ever." Birbach didn't concede the suggestion was worthwhile, but a few hours later some remarks he made indicated to me that he would think about what I had said—carefully.

After an hour or so, Jerry decided that I was not about to be specific with him, and so he put a proposition to me. He said that in his opinion the only acceptable solution would be garden apartments exclusively for the elderly. I told him that in my judgment if he was sincere about that position, then he ought to start looking around for a new neighborhood. He became a bit irritated and asked me to "come back with an offer." It was as though we were there to haggle over a piece of real estate. I told him I was not there to bargain but only to explore. I told him frankly that I doubted the project could even be reduced as much as 50 percent. Wunderman, who had not said much up to that point, first indicated displeasure with that comment, but then when I repeated that I did not think they should reasonably expect anything like what Jerry was asking, Wunderman said, "Remember, we are starting at the bottom and working up, you are starting at the top and working down." I told Wunderman that I was not starting anywhere but at the end.

Throughout the three or four hours we were together, Wunderman and Birbach tried to figure out whether I was serious or simply very slow in my "bargaining." By the time the night was over I'm sure they were convinced I was serious.

There is no doubt that the vacancy rate has gone up in the area, nor do I think there is any question that a sizable number of residents will move out if the project is built as now proposed. The objective really is to keep that number down to the minimum and here the F.H.R.A. can be helpful. There is no point in trying to satisfy them completely; that cannot be done. The approach should be to anticipate their opposition to whatever plan is announced and then to overcome it with an articulate predominant opinion from other segments of the community.

It was a helpful talk.

If this were only a matter of weighing the practical strengths of the two positions it would be easy to resolve. The opponents have no "legal" strength. They have exhausted the courts and the Legislature and they are now at the mercy of the mayor. But the matter is not that simple. The fact is that there is much common sense in the arguments being made by the Forest Hills residents. Whether we like it or not, the fact that people will move out (even if they are "wrong" in so doing) is one that must be contended with. If the project is built and large numbers of residents move out, they will not be replaced by middle-class people but will be substituted for by other low-income and welfare people, and that will be the beginning of the crawling blight that has affected other middle-income areas of this town. That must be prevented—if possible.

Birbach is leaving for Florida tomorrow and will not be back until the twenty-fifth. He asked me to put off my report until then, and I could not resist telling him how strange I thought that suggestion was in view of his public statement that I was already unforgivably late. I told him I would not wait for him but that I would give Marty Wunderman a copy of my report when it was ready.

Thursday, July 13, 1972

Seymour Samuels called. He said he wanted to "clear the air."

I think the most significant thing Samuels said was that whatever happened, he and his group, unlike Birbach, would stand and fight to keep the community intact. All Samuels wants is a "reasonable opportunity" to sell the project. In the course of the conversation Samuels insisted upon getting into the reasons for his group's lack of confidence in me at the outset. He pointed out that someone in the mayor's office had told him even before my name was announced that a compromise had been worked out. He said that he has heard that several times from various sources, including the press. I told Samuels it wasn't true and that it was getting so bad I found it almost amusing. In any event, I think he is now convinced that at least we're trying to do something.

Samuels felt that cutting the project in half and making one building Mitchell-Lama might be salable. I told him I was sure it would be salable to Forest Hills, but I didn't think it would be to the other side of the issue. I dropped the suggestion of three 18's, one of which would be Mitchell-Lama and pointed out that they would bring down the low-income to approximately the same number as Latimer Gardens. He said that would be almost impossible "to sell." I'm sure that he will circulate the idea and get back to me on Monday. Their communications system is working very well; when he called me at about 10:30 this morning he was fully up to date on my meeting with Birbach that had ended at about one o'clock this morning.

Samuels said one thing that was encouraging. I explained that I was late with my report largely because I had spent "too much time" with the Forest Hills people. He felt that the time was well spent because I had finally been able—by virtue of a persistent "devil's advocate" approach—to create a "psychology of compromise." That's gratifying.

Judge Milton Mollen was the judge again today. He is the only person I have spoken to concerning my tentative conclusions. His intelligence, his candor, and his vast knowledgeability on matters political and governmental are invaluable. He let me ramble, then moved in—he was cogent, precise, encouraging. His theme (and he seems to agree with my approach): "Keep it honest"; "Damn the torpedoes"; "You're going to get shot down no matter what you say, so say exactly what you think." He also had some advice about the mechanics of releasing the report. He felt that it should be shown first to the mayor, and the mayor should have an opportunity to react. Conceivably, the mayor's suggestions will be acceptable to me; if they aren't, nothing can prevent me from rejecting them. I'll call the mayor's office and tell them that's what I'll do.

George Douris called to say he's doing a story for the Sunday *Long Island Press*. He has an awful lot of information he didn't get from me—most of it accurate. I've heard rumors that the *New York Times* is doing one on Monday.

Patrolman DeMuro of the 112th Precinct called. He's the community relations officer and in that capacity he has numerous programs for youth, basketball, bowling, judo, trips, etc. He feels the program is well suited to the type of youth one might expect in the projects.

In going through my files on Corona tonight, I found some general notes on city government which rang a bell. The present situation and others we've been in, like Corona and Willets Point, were all extraordinary but had a number of elements in common. One thing that strikes me is that in each of these cases the eventual solution was basically generated not by government but by people outside of government. In Corona it was our compromise plan. In Willets Point it was our ability to persuade Tom Hoving, who at that time had not yet been appointed parks commissioner. And now in Forest Hills—if there is to be a solution—it will be at least in part the result of this unusual if not unique independent agency. One has to wonder why this needed to be so. Surely government was capable of making these judgments unaided. Perhaps what's needed is some kind of agency or office designed particularly to anticipate, prevent or, if necessary, adjust problems of this type. The ombudsman notion comes as close to any as I can think of offhand, and it's an idea that has been attractive to a lot of people for a long time.

Every time we are called upon in situations like Glen Oaks, the Little Neck Marina, the Lefrak case, and most recently the Schermerhorn Street urban renewal, I'm reminded how unfair it is that the community is required to pay for its defense against government errors. In many of these situations, if we had charged a fair fee the communities would have been effectively denied representation. Why shouldn't government provide at the tax-payers' expense a community counsel fully staffed and with subpoena power? Given the right to subpoena, many of these problems would probably be solved long before they reach the critical stages. Actually the Department of Investigation was originally designed to perform this role, but since that agency is totally beholden to the mayor it is not free to operate as objectively as it might. Moreover, as a practical matter, in recent years it has become limited to criminal activity.

Apparently the only reason why efforts to create an ombudsman have been rejected is the politicians' fear that the office might make

them vulnerable. Then, too, there would be a continuing temptation for anyone serving as ombudsman to gallop into the mayor's
office on the broad back of his white steed. But I think it is true that
people are more and more fed up with "politicians" and it is just
possible that an effort at getting this kind of idea implemented
might be successful within the next few years. It's worth trying.

Friday, July 14, 1972

I met with Haberman of HUD again this morning and got some
refined knowledge about the cutting-down process. One of the
important features that I had not paid sufficient attention to earlier
is the possibility that the money freed by the reduction in the
construction might be devoted to other housing (such as Section
23) for Queens. I have a call in to Green to confirm this on
Monday.

I went from HUD to Deputy Mayor Hamilton's office. He was
there with Nat Leventhal, Dave McGregor, Hamilton's assistant,
and Steve Isenberg of the mayor's office. I gave them a discursive
treatment of the problem, and without telling them the ultimate
conclusion (which indeed I do not fully have), I suggested various
possibilities as to cutting down. They're not too happy, particularly
since they think I have nothing to offer the blacks. I told them that
at least for the time being I would not recommend building
elsewhere in Queens anything like 430 units. I told them I would
try to get a report to the mayor by next Thursday or Friday and
that I would give him an opportunity to react to it before it became
public. I explained to Hamilton that I would like the mayor to have
the chance to correct or otherwise make suggestions about the
contents of the report, but that in the end if I couldn't accept the
recommendations, the report should be published as I wrote it.
Hamilton thought that was fair.

I later spoke to the mayor and he agreed. Hamilton summarized
our previous discussion and emphasized that we would have to go
back to the Board of Estimate. The mayor does not seem to be
particularly concerned about that.

The mayor has been true to his earlier assurance that I would be permitted to remain "independent." I pointed out to him that I thought this worked two ways: I expected that he would disagree with parts of my report and he might even reject it *in toto*. He said that could happen, but we would have to wait to see.

Contact was made with both the *News* and *Times* today and arrangements are being made for me to talk to the editorial boards of both papers sometime next week after the report is prepared.

I must begin dictating this weekend. The missing pieces will have to fall in while we're writing. I must keep in mind that the mayor ought to be presented not only with my suggestions but with a listing of other alternatives.

Today I made a recheck of my information with the architect Sam Paul and HUD and city officials. But I'm still not sure I have all the pieces.

To make matters really worse, we have no air conditioning, no water, and only limited lighting at the office, thanks to Con Ed's latest brown-out. Everything in this building is direct current—including the pumps. I'm hoping I'll be able to persuade one of the girls to stay tomorrow anyway because I must start dictating.

Saturday, July 15, 1972

I know at least generally where I will have to go with the report. It's difficult to imagine that the city has ever had a more complex local problem. There are so many considerations to take into account, and in many cases the considerations, while valid, are at cross-purposes with other equally valid ones. Solomon's problem was an easier one: all he had to ascertain was which of the harlots was lying to him. We found a number of liars here, but that didn't solve the problem.

There is one thing everyone seems to agree on—the severity of the ghetto problem, and that something must be done about it. Even the Forest Hills community will concede that; common sense, which they have in abundance, makes the conclusion inevitable. Their feeling is not that the problem should not be alleviated, but rather that this project will not help solve the problem, and will in fact make it worse by simply spreading the blight. There is much to what they say. There are not many—not even Golar—who make convincing arguments for large-scale institutional housing as a solution. On the other hand, none of the other devices such as Section 23 dispersal, are now practical; the real estate industry and the federal maximum rent levels make it nearly useless for large-scale relocation. Since the law now mandates some form of dispersal, it's a matter of selecting the best of poor alternatives.

If one were starting from scratch, the problem would not be so difficult. This is the wrong site—given its cost and all the other various problems—but it would not be reasonable to attempt to undo this whole project at this point. To begin with, the cost would be exorbitant. And perhaps more decisive than the money involved would be the psychological and precedential impact of such a decision. It would mean that no community in the future could reasonably be asked to participate in a dispersal program; all would be able to point to Forest Hills and to demand similar treatment as a matter of fairness.

On the other hand, the project cannot be left as it is. Not only because the fear must be assuaged, but because the present size of the project threatens the potential tenants themselves. As it now stands, this project's dimensions will make it difficult if not impossible to have any kind of meaningful assimilation. Thus, for the sake of the low-income sector who will live in Forest Hills this project should be reduced. The low-income sector will never accept this proposition nor even believe that it can be sincerely offered, but it is nevertheless clear to me that it's true.

So the question becomes: How much smaller and in what composition? Here the practicalities intrude. Legally, the reduction could not be accomplished unless Golar can be persuaded to do it. How far can one reasonably ask Golar to go? My own guess is that he and the mayor are hoping for a reduction of no more than six stories on each building with perhaps a middle-income mix worked into the project of that size. I do not believe that's enough of a reduction, and I'm sure the community would not think so either. The HUD figures indicate that we can go to 12 stories with an additional $2.4 million equity contribution by the city. Hamilton has told me that by virtue of recent fiscal changes the city could produce $3 million.

If reduced to 12 stories the project would be compatible, generally, with the Latimer Gardens property, which, so far as one can now tell, has proven to be fairly successful. If reduced to 12, I think the population should be totally low-income with the proportions as set forth at present: 40 percent of the units for elderly low-income and 60 percent of the units for straight family low-income. Certainly, mix is a good idea, but I'm sure Golar wouldn't accept a dilution of the low-income units to a number less than half, and there is no point in recommending a compromise which Golar is bound to reject, and which, therefore, will be totally useless. That would simply leave the status quo of three 24's, which would be tragic.

Three 12's at the present population ratios is the conclusion. There are criteria and I believe it to be reasonable. I think the conclusion could probably be defended against all attacks, but I'm still leery about presenting it. While I think the report can be written persuasively enough to rationalize the conclusion to an intelligent reader, I'm sure that the suggestion of anything like 50 percent will be regarded by offhand observers as a simple cop-out. No one will believe that it was anything other than arbitrary. It also presents a serious problem with respect to the mayor's position. Even assuming that he's somehow politically motivated (and only God and the mayor would know to what extent), he, perhaps as well as anybody in this town, is sensitive to the ghetto problem and knows its vast and dire implications. That sensitivity and knowledge will make it very difficult for him to go as far as the reduction I am thinking of. On the other side, I'm sure that once the community is told of three 12's they will probably be surprised that this much of a reduction was recommended, but instead of accepting it, their experience as businessmen and bargainers will tell them to demand more. They will no doubt ask for more elderly at least, and probably will demand total elderly.

On all sides, therefore, there are questions and problems, but I've heard every view, weighed every consideration many times, and the three 12's seems to me the best of many danger-fraught positions. It remains to be seen whether the powers will agree.

Tuesday and Wednesday, July 18 and 19

The fates conspire against us! A heat wave—and another brown-out. A *dark* brown-out. No air conditioning, no switchboard, and no running water—not even johns for two whole days. It was almost impossibly hot, particularly today. I've been working in a T-shirt. Despite it, we've managed to dictate fifty-two rough draft pages. I'll write the rest of the draft out tomorrow morning, then try pushing it into final form. It hurts doing it this way because the language will be so important, but there's no choice. I must get it to the mayor's designees by Friday afternoon. It should be released on Monday.

Koch called. He'd like a copy before release so that he can prepare his own. Gold, too.

Saturday, July 22, 1972

Two girls put together a final rough draft and I met with the mayor, Hamilton, Eisenberg, Tom Morgan, the mayor's P.R. man, and Kriegel to give them an opportunity to review it. They did—they're all unhappy, I think, but none of them attempted to push me. Some of the points they made will call for language changes. I think it was good to talk to them, but I'm sure I've made them uncomfortable.

Matty Troy called me long distance from somewhere out West where he's working on the McGovern campaign (who would have believed it?). He had heard from Breslin that I was about to report and wanted to know if he could help. I told him what I was thinking of and how his help could be important. He agreed to support the proposal. He's always been a good friend and proved it again today.

I worked on the draft later in the afternoon.

Sunday, July 23, 1972

Except for Channel 13's Fischer–Spassky analysis I spent the day working through the draft and making minor corrections. I've had it—I think we have to go with it as is.

Monday, July 24, 1972

Draft to the printer. Galleys tomorrow. Release Wednesday—and then we'll see.

Wednesday, July 26, 1972

My report (see Appendix) was filed with the mayor, Board of Estimate, and City Council this morning. A couple of hours later there was a press conference at which I answered questions. I was reluctant to have the conference; my thought was that if I could avoid it I would force the media to read the report. Professionals like Bob Laird of the City Hall P.R. staff and Dick Aurelio pointed out that in all likelihood they would not read the report carefully and they convinced me that it would be a safer course for me to attempt to summarize it. I did, and answered a dozen or so questions.

Matty Troy issued a statement immediately after the press conference. He was true to his word. His position is a powerful, unequivocal endorsement of the plan as proposed. It has to be a big help. Manes has apparently decided to hang back. I suspect he will try to come in with something different; probably a mix at twelve stories. I think that's too much of a reduction unless he parlays it with ironclad assurances that he will supply other sites in Queens. The mayor has not approved the report and probably won't, at least for a while. The press conference this morning revealed the antagonism that the report will draw from the black population. One of the black reporters and I had a talk. It is simply impossible to convince him that the Jewish opposition is not largely racist. I disagree with him. It's clear to me that the objection is to crime and deterioration and not color. The coincidence that most of the lower economic class are black is what produces confusion. This isn't casuistry, but the black leadership is sure to say it is.

The mayor has not approved of the report. Unless pressure comes from other sources, the mayor will simply not move the compromise. The sources must be from Queens, and that means Manes now that Troy has already spoken. We are bound to get opposition from Golar and it will probably be strong. I hope he reads the report first.

In the end, the report does not state the whole truth. For example, I have made no mention of the numerous blacks who condemn the project because I would have to do it without mentioning their names and that would have left us open to a "fraud" charge. Nor does it contain the actual vacancy rate in Forest Hills which has reached a dangerous pitch. To have mentioned it would have been to risk a panic. These, I guess, were political judgments, although a politician would probably call it some high form of prudence.

Now that the report has been filed, the struggle is almost purely political, and that is perhaps the most depressing aspect of all. There is a good likelihood that this problem will not be resolved on the hard facts and the soundness of the arguments but rather in terms of who can muster the greater pressure. Everybody in town is working now. Politicians are talking to one another trying to figure out the safest bet. Proselytizing is going on with the various Jewish and community groups. Editorial boards are talking to their reporters. Out of all of this will come varying consensus opinions. The politicians will weigh them by their own scales and will decide accordingly.

Saturday, July 29, 1972

Immediately after publication of the report, Golar and Birbach blasted it. That was predictable. Samuels, Grunblatt and company are trying to talk Manes into an all elderly or a mix at 12 stories.

That was also predictable. I've been telling Manes and anyone else who will listen that it's still not certain the mayor will go to 12, let alone any further dilution. I've been warning them that if they take the position that 12 is not enough, the mayor could simply say that since my proposal *does not* ensure receptivity by the community, there's no point in going to the trouble and expense of the compromise. I think this is getting through to Manes, but he's reluctant to live with it. He apparently feels that he must come up with something different from my report. He's told me as much. As Queens' principal officeholder—largely dependent upon a Jewish vote—it's a must.

Birbach called. Before he issued his blast he casually noted that he hadn't even bothered to read the report. I sent him one.

The *Daily News* gave us a favorable editorial, as have the *Long Island Press* and the *Times*. All three said clearly that the proposal should be adopted. This is almost more than I expected.

In addition to the Anti-Defamation League of B'nai B'rith, Ed Koch and Senator Gold have all been quoted as favoring the report. What we need now is Manes. Matty Troy actually was the first to speak in support and he did so powerfully. But contrary to the popular assumption, it does not appear that Manes automatically agrees with Troy. At least he hasn't come along, so far.

The mayor has left the city. Manes was complaining about the mayor being away while he was fighting it out with his people. He also said that he was going away himself for two weeks, and everything would have to wait until he returned. I told him that might kill all chance for a compromise. I called Hamilton, explained, and asked if he could get the mayor to talk to Manes. He said he would.

Tuesday, August 1, 1972

Matty Troy continues to bang away in favor of the proposal. WINS came out in favor of it last night. But today both Herbert Kahn and Andre Ferenzo, a candidate for the State Senate against Gold, came out against it. Kahn said it "would satisfy no one."

Saturday, August 12, 1972

For the most part, the events of the last eleven days are described in the various news clippings.

A great deal, however, has been going on behind the scenes. The mayor decided to hang back until he saw how the plan was received and what kind of pressure would be mounted. Golar has been strong. Birbach is effectively isolating himself. Manes is the key. The QJCC thinks they'll be able to come away with something more "acceptable" than the compromise. Manes has taken an ambivalent position. Meanwhile, the project is being built.

Monday, August 14, 1972

Golar came out with his own plan on Sunday: "Leave the buildings at 24, sell one off for middle income." Roger Starr's group came out simultaneously with a plan to convert the entire project into Mitchell-Lama, 20 percent low-income. The newspapers tried to reach me on Sunday but couldn't. They finally got me this morning and I told them:

1. I thought it was "hopeful" that Golar would consider compromise.

2. Both their plans had been considered and rejected during our study because the project would be too large.

3. The Golar and Starr estimates of the per unit costs of my plan are unrealistically high unless there is further extensive delay.

I spoke with Kriegel who told me the mayor had reached Manes in Tel Aviv on Saturday. Manes told him he was going to ask for a mix at 12. The mayor is considering coming out for my report on Friday. I don't envy the mayor's position here. What an obscenely difficult job he has!

Saturday, August 19, 1972

It took more than three weeks, but this afternoon the mayor announced his support for the "Cuomo Compromise." It was a hard decision and, honestly viewed, it would have to be regarded as a courageous one. More important, he has somehow managed to get Golar to go along with him. Golar has agreed—very reluctantly—to submit the proposal to the Board of Estimate. Now, of course, we'll get the Queens view. There seems to be no way Manes can avoid making his own position clear at this point. The buck finally stopped with the mayor. I think it would have made more sense for Queens to have spoken first, but after a lot of foot shuffling, John got stuck for the drinks.

If history is any indication, Manes will announce that he is disappointed with the mayor's position, but is forced—reluctantly—to accept it. I can't imagine his saying that he would prefer a mix even if it meant going up a few more floors. Size is still the major irritant.

Birbach, of course, loves it—it gives him something to be heard on. The worst thing that could happen to Jerry would be for this matter to resolve itself, driving him back to insufferable anonymity.

Golar is in a tough position. Having given up his hard ground by suggesting his own compromise, he lost much of the "logic" of his position. The difference between his new compromise and mine is only 130 low-income units; it's hard to make the argument that such a difference defines the moral distinction between a "liberal" and a "bigot."

The cost factor remains a problem—much worse now than it was when I reported, because of the delay. But if some strong sentiment for compromise can be demonstrated in the next week or so, the financial problem can be sublimated.

The media are banging it out now. It's frightening how important they are. Depending upon the extent of their investigation, the quotes they select, and the emphasis they give, public opinion can go one way or the other. It will be interesting to see how they handle it.

It's still too early for a "retrospective," but I can't help thinking that the compromise effort has, at least, elevated the dialogue to a more acceptable level, intellectually and by decibel count. Now the argument is addressed to specific variations; previously it was almost totally a clash of emotions, symbols, and generalizations.

Unfortunately, we've never been able to get anyone to do a full version of the report for general distribution. That would have helped a great deal. Whether or not one agrees with its contents, disagreement would require specifics. That would be helpful here. The fact is that very few people, even on the Board of Estimate and City Council, are taking the time to read the copies of the report they've been given. Why bother with the facts?

Monday, August 28, 1972

Out of the office for a week but not away from Forest Hills. Things continue to happen rapidly—mostly expressions of opinion from various groups. Today a number of "liberal" organizations released a statement condemning the mayor for having adopted the compromise proposal. Like so many other allegedly "liberal" pronunciamientos this one appeared to be primitively absolutist. It referred to the compromise as a "kissing of the feet of the Forest Hills racist." I can't believe that's a fair or even intelligent appraisal. The total difference in units for low-income between the proposal accepted by the mayor and the Golar plan is 130. The compromise specifically calls for making up many more than this number of units in other parts of Queens. Manes has agreed to that In fact, it seems clear to me that the best way to prevent other scatter-site developments would be to insist on the three 24's.

Why then, the strident protest? It's symbolistic, as has been much of the argument. Any reduction is regarded as a surrender of principle. But what is the principle? *That the rights of the poor should be advanced.* Fine, the proposal does that—it is designed to make this project work for the poor. *That the earlier decision should be respected as the product of the governmental system's operation.* Does this mean the liberal cause despises change even where error seems to be clear? That sounds more like a "conservative" point of view. *That the desire of the blacks should be fulfilled because they have earned consideration as a result of their victimization by the rest of society.* But what blacks are making the demand for three 24-story towers? Not black project tenants or potential tenants. Not black home owners in Queens. Not black planners like

Knowles. But black "leaders." Is it possible their credentials are not as authentic as Birbach's credentials as a middle-class leader?

The liberals, as reported by the *New York Post*, make one very legitimate point. Had the compromise been greeted with sure evidence that it would stop the flight of the middle class from Forest Hills, it would have been more acceptable as a solution. To date—thanks largely to the natural instinct to exploit advantages and weaknesses—the F.H. community has spent most of its time asking for more. To make this case they have to seize on the principal predicate to my argument—which was that an exodus might occur. But if it will occur even with the compromise, why compromise? The answer, I believe, is that there will be *no* exodus if the compromise is adopted. Unfortunately, unless one has had the kind of extraordinary exposure to the community and its thinking that I've had, there would be no way to know this. But I'm sure that these people are too tough to surrender, particularly since the project as reduced gives them a reasonable chance for success.

The prospects for the immediate future are grim. Three hearings —Community Planning Board, City Planning Commission, and Board of Estimate. Unless our Queens leaders speak up for reason, there will be large numbers of liberals opposed, large numbers of F.H. absolutists opposed and large numbers of "seekers after more" opposed. The board may be left with no intelligent reason for adopting the compromise. I may talk to Samuels about this myself. While I'm not supposed to be an "advocate," it is difficult to stand by and watch what could be a good solution die from mishandling.

I appeared on the *Direct Line* show this morning. It seems to have gone well. I was asked about Beame and Garelik's request for a construction halt and took the position that the request was unwise. Since they have both indicated they might vote against the compromise, why should they urge a halt which would inevitably present delay claims? (I'm not sure either of them thought about that possibility.)

Both of them are almost purely defensive; their principal concern appears to be not to get involved with a hot potato. It's Lindsay's mess, let him take the heat.

Seymour Lachman of the Board of Education called and asked how he could help. I brought him up to date and suggested that the greatest assistance he could offer would be in clarifying for the Jewish community the exact posture of the matter, to wit, the compromise proposal or the status quo. He said he would do what he could.

Kriegel was on the phone this morning. He feels Manes understands the technical position and will make it clear at the community level. He expects that there will nevertheless be a great deal of argument concerning other and different plans not before the board, and he hopes the CPC is not too rigid in ruling against these. He's concerned that the attitude would be considered dogmatic.

A nice question presents itself as to whether I personally should appear at any of the upcoming hearings. One would think that as the author of the proposal it would be pure logic for me to comment. But that presents difficulties. My role was created—and is limited—by the mayor's mandate. Does it extend to "working out" a compromise or just reporting on the facts? Throughout, I've been saying that I was not a mediator in the sense of one who is assigned the task of negotiating a settlement. That would have been impossible because of the time factor, the prolific multiplication of different viewpoints and my lack of political strength. But now that the compromise has been proposed, there appears to be no one else willing to "advocate" it. The mayor's reluctance in accepting it is understandable in view of what he must have been hoping for. Although I've received opinions from many who told me privately that they regard the compromise as a reasonable solution, political considerations drive them into anonymity. Friends have suggested I should appear at the hearings. I'm not so sure. I'm concerned that an attempt by me to argue for the compromise would appear to impeach its objectivity in the public's eye, and that can be harmful to the proposal's chances. It seems to me that for the time being it would be wiser simply to wait and see whether I'm invited to appear and speak.

Later today Joe DeVoy called to invite me to the Community

Board meeting. He said he was not sure if he wanted me to speak, but wanted me to be present. I told him I would be there.

Wednesday, August 30, 1972

I spoke to Lashinsky. He insists that his group will get a better solution by resisting the compromise and by demanding that the project be converted into all elderly units. I pointed out that redesign would be extremely expensive; that Golar could not possibly accept that proposal and, therefore, it could not be put before the Board of Estimate; and that the project exclusively for the elderly would be a sell-out, particularly in constitutional terms. I explained to him the difficulties even now being experienced by the Town of Hempstead. Lashinsky told me that they have contacted somebody in the administration who they feel will be responsive to them.

I agreed with Lashinsky on one point. From what I have seen, it does appear that the projected cost figures are being "jacked up." Perhaps Golar is simply being conservative or, conceivably, he is building a case for himself. In any event, I've asked the mayor's office to get me a copy of Golar's description of the projected costs as communicated to the City Planning Commission. They are eager for me to avoid a running debate with Golar over the numbers and I told him I would try to do so subject to changing events.

Thursday, August 31, 1972

I spoke with Aurelio today. He is busy trying to put his restaurant together* but, as always, found time to give advice. Apparently a number of rabbis from the area have asked for an opportunity to talk to him: he must be the man Lashinsky was talking about. Because he's no longer part of the administration, he felt reluctant to meet with them. I thought he could be helpful. Obviously, since they had reached out for him they regard his opinion as worthwhile. That means he has a chance to explain the realities and to

---

* Jimmy's on West 52nd Street in New York City.

convince them. The rabbis specifically rejected D.A.'s suggestion that I come along to any meeting. This is understandable too. I'm in no position to ask for anything more than I've already recommended, so that there is no point in their trying to do business with me.

What a curious situation. I'm convinced that most people would regard the compromise as reasonable; I'm sure that Forest Hills would prefer three 12's to three 24's. I even suspect, after having talked last week to Reverend Tim Mitchell, one of the leaders of the proponents, that the blacks who oppose the compromise would not be terribly unhappy with it, but are making their argument to make sure that nothing worse than the compromise occurs. And yet there is a likelihood that the relatively small percentage of people who will be represented at the hearing will speak negatively. The failing is with the system, but here as in many cases, the difficulty is in trying to find something better.

Tuesday, September 5, 1972

Golar appeared on the *Direct Line* show Sunday morning. He's in a difficult position. He tried hard to make it clear that he was not responsible for the original site selection and was just operating as a good soldier in advancing the compromise. This ambivalence, coupled with the toe dance he must perform in order to object to the compromise while at the same time submitting it to the Board of Estimate, makes him come off as confused. He's not. At all times he's totally in command of himself and his thinking, but is in the unfortunate position of having to defer to his superior's commands. It must hurt.

Wednesday, September 6, 1972

The big news yesterday was Manes' most recent position.

Manes started by telling me even before the report that he would have to come up with something different. His first attempt was to suggest a mix. He soon found that was an impossible position because, as we predicted, Golar would not mix at 12 and the community would not go to the 17 or 18 floors that would be needed. His next position was to make the project either exclusively for the elderly or at least increase the number of elderly units substantially. This was apparently shot down by the arguments we made to Lashinsky. Now, finally he is talking about converting the entire project, as reduced by my proposal, into a cooperative.

In the course of my study I concluded that the cooperative would not work because it would threaten the number of elderly, since they don't have the potential upward economic mobility, and also because "sweat equity" is not a practicable concept when you are dealing with spanking-new apartment buildings. This proposal, like so many others, is theoretically attractive but has practical flaws. It could put Manes in the contradictory position of arguing against the inclusion of the elderly.

The cooperative aspect, attractive in notion, could come closer to reality if Manes could get HUD to bend a few guidelines. Of course, since I had no political authority or base, I was in no position to make demands. Manes—particularly if he could get Golar's support—might be able to do it. And Golar has expressed an interest in the idea of a cooperative. Its principal attractiveness is that it creates, if nothing more, the illusion of proprietary interest. Owners are apt to be more careful than tenants about their property. It also would call for a board of directors from the community who, while having no technical power to control the project, would at least have a good vehicle for community input.

The objective is quite clear. All the suggestions are aimed at producing a less "dangerous" population for the project. It is thought the cooperative would provide greater tenant-selection possibilities.

Wednesday, September 13, 1972

The first of the three hearings was held last night; in a number of ways it was unlike any Community Planning Board hearing I had ever attended. By my count, some nine hundred people were there. While a number of speakers became quite emotional, the hearing was orderly overall. It went until well past midnight with some seventy speakers. Only two spoke in favor of the compromise; the others unanimously opposed it.

"Confused" is perhaps the best word to describe the meaning of what took place last night. Insofar as the hearing demonstrates a strong position against any project, it was by no means a surprise, but it's not reasonable to think that these people were saying that the compromise offered them so little, they would just as soon accept the status quo. Their feeling is they have the compromise; they are trying to improve upon it. They have simply not been convinced that their negative posture might jeopardize the compromise proposal. The mechanics are beyond them, and their political instinct is that the mayor and the city simply would not have the guts to permit the status quo to remain no matter what occurs.

Curiously, most of the references yesterday were to the "Lindsay" compromise and not the "Cuomo" plan. If it had been deemed acceptable they probably would have called it the "Community" plan.

I didn't speak. Neither did any representative of the Borough President's office, Senator Gold or Ben Rosenthal. The board took the position that since the senator did not live in the district, he would not be permitted to speak. My guess is that this position did not displease Gold.

Thursday, September 14, 1972

The publicity which followed the Community Planning Board hearing continues to describe the event as "a denunciation" of the compromise plan. I wonder how many people in the city understand what is happening. One of the leaders of an opposition group said to me Tuesday night—I thought gloatingly—that they had "sandbagged" the mayor. They had gotten word to him that if he accepted the compromise they would go along with it. They never had any intention of doing so. It was a classic case of fraud in the inducement, but then almost everybody actively engaged in the political game-playing appears to regard that kind of tactic as permissible, if not *de rigueur*. That kind of sophistication is disheartening, but increasingly it appears naïve to believe it could be any other way. Having sandbagged the mayor, the opposition is now convinced that they have him in a box. They're trying to get Beame, Garelik, and Leone to vote down the compromise in the belief that they can push Lindsay to the wall. I don't agree it will work, but there's no point in trying to convince them.

And on the matter of trying to convince anybody, Paul Sandman stopped by today at the office; he told me that there was a growing sentiment in the community that my persistence in commenting on the maneuvering was creating an impression that I had an undisclosed and probably venal interest. What concerns me is that this attitude jeopardizes the already dubious prospects for the compromise, and so prudence dictates that we stay out of the brawl. It might even be best if I don't show up at the City Planning Commission hearing.

Professor Paul Graziano from St. John's University School of Law was generous in praise of the report. More and more I regret that we were not able to publish the entire text. Even Rabbi Grunblatt and Joe DeVoy publicly commended the text of the report at the Community Board hearing. But so few have read it. It might have been a different ball game if we could have relied on the actual document instead of the highly truncated newspaper descriptions of it. Conceivably—although it's not likely—we could get someone to run it before the Board of Estimate meeting.

Friday, September 15, 1972

Joe DeVoy called: he issued his release at twelve noon; his Community Board voted unanimously to reject the original proposal, to reject the compromise and to demand that the mayor work with them toward something else. Specifically, that something else would be elderly and vets, exclusively. DeVoy admits they're gambling—they've been told the mayor will come in. I don't think so, particularly in view of his having been stung again yesterday in Harbor Village when the Board of Estimate voted to kill that middle-income project.

Now where are we? Given the manner in which the meeting was arranged it was inevitable that the vote would be negative. I would suspect that the City Planning Commission will approve the compromise. The Board of Estimate will be purely political. And the political considerations are beyond me. The mayor, I think, will stand fast—it will be the compromise or the original project. His liberal instincts were strong enough to make even the compromise hard to take; I doubt that he'll be driven any further than he has been already. Everyone else on the board—other than Sutton and Connor* evidently—are mayoralty candidates, and each will probably read the situation in that framework. After Harbor Village, it may even be that they will go for broke and try to kill the whole project. I don't believe that can be done legally, but there seems to be little patience with the law in this situation.

A number of people have called to say that they didn't consider the Community Planning Board decision—or the hearing—to be representative. I told them the only thing they could do about that was to show up at the City Planning Commission on the twentieth and provide the city with what they believed was truly reflective of the community view.

The story, I'm sure, will be different there. The liberal segment will be out in force—this strong position by the Community Board will—according to Reverend Tim Mitchell's prediction—compel the other side to the controversy to come out with equal or greater strength. I continue to believe that in the end the competing forces will lead most reasonable people to the middle ground—driven by good sense and not expediency. But the question remains whether reasonableness or expediency will prevail at the Board of Estimate.

Saturday, September 16, 1972

So many questions are produced by this situation that volumes would be needed to explore them all. Breslin raised one of them today in talking about the Jewish vote. He's convinced that it will go to McGovern as it traditionally does to the Democratic candidate. The publicity indicates it will either go to Nixon or at least will not go so strongly Democratic as it has in the past. I'm

---

* Robert Connor, borough president of Richmond County (Staten Island).

inclined to believe that in New York it will move to the right, despite the historical repugnance to that direction, and Forest Hills illustrates one of the reasons. The middle-class Jew in this town shares the concerns and fears of the middle class generally. What Jewish history teaches about the danger of strong movements to central government and diminishment of individual rights takes a back seat to the impact of immediate problems. Crime, a growing resentment of welfare, increasing taxes, the fear of an increasing black population, all combine to move the Jew—and the rest of the middle class—away from the liberal point of view and toward whatever else is available. This has certainly not been lost on the politicians. Almost without exception the most prominent candidates for the mayoralty seem to be reacting. Lindsay has moved toward the middle. His recent emphasis on the crime problem, welfare controls, and his Forest Hills position point up the move. Koch is not the liberal he was two years ago. Blumenthal is talking about "law and order" and now concentrates on the crime problem. A few years ago any attempt to concentrate on crime as an issue would have been regarded by the liberals as a covert attack on the blacks. Now everyone discusses it. Putting aside the motivation, the emphasis is a reasonable one—at least it has the virtue of being appropriate; there's no question that crime is the big problem and must be dealt with.

And crime is only one of many. Housing—which suffers too from the "crime" problem—schooling, taxes, transportation, the whole urban crisis.

I think that as long as the city is structured as it is, no individual or group of individuals is sufficient to the task. The structure must be altered. The Charter Revision Commission set up by the Legislature is still dormant. Here, too, there are probably political considerations that must be dealt with. The mayor has already announced his choice, but the governor has deliberately delayed in implementing the legislation. That's unfortunate. Some change is necessary.

It's discouraging when one considers the huge amount of time, attention, and energy that have been spent in this situation not to resolve the problem but to achieve a political advantage. The posturing, the feinting, the set-ups and the scheming. I suspect if men of good will had spent the same time and energy thinking purely about a solution, we would have been out of this mess by now.

Another thing occurs to me about the Community Planning Board's decision. Newspaper accounts stressed that the board was "resentful" that it was being given the proposal on a take-it-or-leave-it basis. That's an interesting reaction—it's like the man who's broke finding out someone is willing to give him money, and then being resentful because he wasn't consulted on precisely how much and in what form. The community seems to have forgotten that at the time the mayor announced the fact-finding expedition, the community had nothing—not even hope! But then, why should this situation be any different from life generally?

Thursday, September 21, 1972

In fifteen years I've been through many City Planning Commission and Board of Estimate hearings. Some of them were unpleasant, but none were so distasteful, if not sickening, as yesterday's hearing before the Planning Commission.

Normally, the City Planning Commission's function is a dubious one. Being composed entirely of mayoral appointees, the permanent suspicion is that they are inevitably reflective of the Executive will. While there have been exceptions from time to time, history provides a sound basis for the suspicion. Particularly was that the case here. The mayor, having adopted the compromise and having pushed Golar into advancing it, it was difficult to imagine the City Planning Commission rejecting the proposal. The media so stated repeatedly before the hearing and Marty Gallent went on record in support of the compromise a couple of weeks ago. This kind of ambivalence—on the one hand, a representation to the public that the hearing will be true and meaningful, and on the other, the concessions that early judgments have been made—shake the confidence and corrupt the process. But this isn't the fault of Marty or the commissioners; it's essentially a weakness in the system. I've pointed it up on many occasions in the past as an advocate;

Birbach didn't miss the opportunity to do the same thing yesterday. His entire presentation and that of his colleagues were sarcastic and cynical.

Other ambivalences contribute to the inefficacy of this hearing process. The commission regularly represents that it wishes the greatest possible community involvement, but just as regularly it ignores the stated judgment of the Community Board. One who is honest in his analysis would have to admit that the extremes on this issue, that is, total community control or total disdain for local sentiment, are equally unacceptable. However, as this entire experience has shown so well, the reasonable position which is so often the middle one, appears to have little salability. The polar positions are the easier ones to take. They have the virtue of simplicity and sometimes even of passion. There should be more community input short of total control. That's the simple truth, but characteristically, yesterday, the community argument was, "We ought to have our way because this problem affects us in Forest Hills immediately." This proposition is neither sound nor tolerable. The issue is obviously citywide, but there was no one yesterday who was able to say that clearly or loudly enough to be able to register. There is an obvious warning here for anyone who's paying attention. It points up the danger in any total decentralization of governmental power in the city.

Another painful contradiction takes the form of the commission's attempt to give "everyone" a full chance to speak in a situation where the proliferation of speakers, the brevity of alloted time, the lack of prepared materials and the inability to control audience reaction all join together to make intelligent discussion impossible. Even the physical facts conspire against effective hearings. The room is too small; dozens and sometimes hundreds are required to wait outside. No selectivity is exercised. Repetition *ad nauseam* occurs at every hearing. The length of the hearings on controversial matters makes it impossible for a commissioner to sit attentively throughout the entire hearings. After a few hours the commissioners come and go in the midst of presentations to attend to whatever biological, professional or political obligations press in on them. This is not lost on the audience.

All of this militated against the chance for an intelligent session yesterday. But there was a great deal more that doomed the hearing. The Forest Hills community is convinced that their principal weapon now, as it has been for the past few months, is to persuade the city fathers and the public at large that it is impossible to expect tolerance and acceptance on the part of the community. To do this they exaggerate their force and resistance. And what is initially in part a pose then communicates itself and feeds on itself and eventually the illusion becomes reality. Yesterday the hundred or so Forest Hills residents who screamed and stomped, cried and shouted, believed what they had earlier pretended to believe.

Birbach's people got to the hearing first and occupied most of the seats. Gold, who has no communication with this group at all, was alone. His "right-minded" people—and I believe there are many of them—have no personal incentive to attend and no organization to inspire them, so that a hundred people spoke for all of Forest Hills. Rosenthal and Koch were absent. Garelik, Manes, and Beame had no representatives. The mayor's office did not appear. There was, in short, only Gold to speak on behalf of the compromise.

The community tactic is now clear beyond any reasonable doubt. This hard core is so hypnotized by what they take to be the effectiveness of their own pressure that they are now convinced that they can push their way to total victory without regard for the nice legalities or administrative procedures. They believe that somehow, someway, if they resist hard enough, a way will be found to kill the project. There is no question in my mind that if they truly believed the choice was between three 24's and three 12's they would accept the three 12's, but they are not prepared to concede that.

Manny Gold was the first to speak, and it became immediately evident that this hearing was to be a Roman circus. His fairness, his intelligence, and his sensitivity all combined were not enough to win him even simple courtesy from the group. He was jeered, booed, cursed, and shouted down. The mob stood drooling with blood in their eyes and turned their thumbs down on the senator who stood alone in the middle of the coliseum. After a while what now appeared to be almost pure hate began turning in on itself.

Assemblyman Herb Miller, whose contentiousness is peerless, drove Joe DeVoy to the point where he had to dissociate himself from him and excoriate him, although they share the same position.

A fracas that erupted in the back of the room and eventually led to Birbach's withdrawal from the meeting in a dramatic gesture was inevitable. It was fortunate it wasn't more severe. The hate boiled over until people had to touch one another violently—a small shove but filled with tons of hate, and small only as a kind of instinctive accommodation to reasonableness and fear.

This was not the community at large; it was the vocal few, but is it fair to ignore the vocal few when the community at large has had its chance and spurned it? What alternative is there to heeding the wishes of those who choose to use the System? How does one reach the community "at large" if it will not speak?

And so yesterday's hundred or so people from Forest Hills screamed no to the compromise, although in fact they prefer it to the original plan. Dozens of blacks and other proponents said no to the compromise, although in fact they prefer it to the Birbach position. The entire hearing seemed to miss the point.

Wednesday, October 4, 1972

The City Planning Commission published its decision and opinions today: 4–2 for the compromise. I was more interested in the rationales than the votes. The majority—Elliott, Rapkin, Coleman, and Gallent—had three opinions. The dissenters—Zuccotti and Michael—one. Elliott's opinion made the point that anything which "may" alleviate the tension is worth trying. Gallent, in a concurring opinion, made intelligent suggestions concerning tenant selection and local option for the future. His idea of permitting the local community to choose among the various methods of scatter-site, e.g., project, mix, Section 23, is particularly appealing. The development of this idea will depend in large measure upon the work of the Charter Revision Commission, which, after a number of recent editorials urging prompt action, was finally launched by the governor yesterday.

Zuccotti's dissent was uninspiring. He thinks it would cost too much. His finishing line was a quote from Emerson to the effect that all compromise is a defeat of principle. Now, John—really! I think his quote is a good deal more vulnerable than was mine from Edmund Burke (see Report, page 200, in Appendix).

No reaction from Forest Hills; they had assumed defeat here. Apparently, however, they have been working effectively with the Board of Estimate. Today's papers had a story indicating that Manes, Leone, Garelik, and Abrams* are all taking a "something more than the Cuomo Compromise is needed" stand. Manes' position and reasons are now clear. As to the others, I'm not sure that they have even read the report. Beame remains aloof—and silent. It should be interesting on the twenty-sixth.

Earlier today I spent nearly two hours with the Synagogue Council. An impressive group. They were interested, intelligent, and generous. At the end of the discussion a motion was made by Rabbi Brickner calling for support of the "Cuomo Compromise." I recommended against their taking a stand now, but suggested that they prepare a position on scatter-site housing to be published after the Forest Hills matter is decided. It seems to me—and I told them this—that something should be done by the Jewish community to rebut the unfair conclusion that Forest Hills proves their bigotry. The conclusion has been arrived at by many, and while it is unfair it is sufficiently prevalent to be worth dealing with. They agreed, and my guess is they will eventually produce a paper that supports the need for some form of scatter-site housing, probably something other than project housing.

Saturday, October 7, 1972

It's been obvious for a long time, and now Forest Hills has brought it into sharp focus, that the "safety in the streets" issue is the single biggest concern of the city at the moment. We have been reduced to the primitive state of worrying not so much about the quality of life as we are about its very preservation! It's no surprise, therefore, to see the candidates lining up for the mayoralty all focusing on

* Robert Abrams, borough president of the Bronx.

this aspect of the platform. Five years ago they would have been called "right-wingers," but now there is no one raising any voice against the "law and order" people. Nor should there be. Undeniably the issue affects everyone and, in fact, it affects most severely those people who would normally be regarded as the principal objects of the liberals' attention. Forest Hills points this up. The critical issue in Forest Hills is the "crime" problem and the fear it's engendered. No amount of sophistry can obscure that. And largely because of the crime and fear, the low-income sector will be deprived of half the proposed units—and if the immediate community has its way, maybe all of them. So the sufferers are the blacks and disadvantaged. (In addition, I'm sure the statistics would show that in terms of actual victimization the ghetto dweller leads the list.)

It seems to me that Reverend Mitchell and his colleagues should in fact be fighting for more law and order, since his people are the most affected. It's not unlike the Italo-American and the Mafia. Every Italo-American pays a price for the Mafia's wrongdoing, no matter how unfair the attribution of guilt; every low-income black is now paying the price for "street violence," no matter how unfair the attribution. The entire scatter-site concept is obstructed, if not defeated, by the fear that low-income blacks mean crime—a fear so powerful that "morality" and "charity" are simply no match for it. Five years ago it might have made sense for the blacks to take the position that an emphasis on law and order was somehow the signal of bigotry and a willingness to permit the oppression of the blacks. We're way past that now. Forest Hills shows clearly that their best position now would be to reorganize and acknowledge the problem, and to join with the rest of the community in a real war on crime. The precise steps to be taken are difficult to find. The problem is so pervasive and many-sided—drugs, the need for police, the failure of the courts and prosecution, poverty—that it's hard to know even where to start. But something must be done. As we said in the Report, we can't afford the luxury of doing nothing while we're waiting for a way of doing everything.

At the very least we ought to start with a firm universal commitment to attack the problem in every way possible, putting to one side the symbolistic treatment which made proponents "law and order bigots" and the others "wide-eyed pseudo-liberals." And above all, the issue must not be permitted to deal with symptoms while leaving the disease to fester. The temptation will be simply to strengthen the police and the courts, and to provide more and better judges, penal institutions, and drug programs. All of this is undeniably necessary. But at the same time we must deal with the ghetto, which grows in size and whose problems increase in intensity. Unless the problem of the poor is solved, we will lock up the muggers today but will be faced with generations of them in the future. We cannot wall off the ghetto and expect it not to explode. If we step back from the problem today and return to the callous neglect of twenty years ago, we may squelch a few assaults and wind up with race riots. I'm afraid politicians will fear that any talk of uplifting and relieving the ghetto problem will be regarded as a relenting on the necessity for more "law and order." We've come, perhaps, full circle. Whereas several years ago many politicians feared discussing law and order because that might mark them as "illiberal," today many will fear to speak the truth about the need for jobs, education, housing, and integration because that might mark them as "permissive." Always the extremes and the pandering to simplistics. I refuse to believe it must be so: there is an intelligent balanced alternative that this town will understand and respect if it is properly and honestly articulated.

Tuesday, October 10, 1972

I spoke with someone at HUD today and he urged me to come in to go over HUD's proposed budget figures. He confirmed what I had suspected; he stated flatly that the Housing Authority's projected cost figures were much too high.

Wednesday, October 25, 1972

Most of the activity for the past two and a half weeks has consisted of semifrenetic negotiating among various groups. Birbach, the Queens Jewish Community Council, and Manes have been back and forth to all of the members of the Board of Estimate, HUD and the Housing Authority in a desperate last-minute effort to wring something more than was offered in my proposal. In the end, Manes was able to persuade Golar and the mayor that the "cooperative" notion, added to my proposal, would make it more palatable. I agree—if it is workable. The theory was designed for situations where there is opportunity for performing substantial work in the form of maintenance and rehabilitation; it would hardly appear to be appropriate here. On the other hand, it's clear—particularly where government is concerned—that where there's a will there's a way. If HUD and the Housing Authority want this thing done they can do it. I hope they will, but I have serious reservations.

One of the aspects of the cooperative that is most appealing to the community is the fact that it provides for a board of directors made up of community representatives. It is apparently being commonly assumed that such a board of directors would have the right to make the ultimate tenant selection. If this were so, it would of course go a long way toward assuaging the community's fears. The language used by the politicians has been loose on the subject, but the impression is given that the board will have absolute power over the choice of tenants.

I'm convinced this is not so and could not be so legally. There is a great danger in not making this clear to the community at large. I've tried to, but the little publicity given my remarks has been lost in the maze of the confusing stories carried by the papers. Curiously, no one appears to be asking the right questions. One would think that members of the Board of Estimate would be analyzing the subject closely and would demand answers to these questions. But that's not happening. Apparently the basic technical matters are regarded as "nitty-gritty," and not worthy of the policy makers' efforts and time. Their judgment will be made in response to different considerations. All of this, therefore, leaves another problem that may not surface for several months. Assuming there is no clarification at the hearing and the cooperative plan is passed, it is conceivable that the cooperative will prove not to be feasible, or that even with a cooperative the Authority will retain control over tenant selection. The disillusioned expectations may cause resentment and another crisis of confidence.

There is a good deal of pressure in the community for even more than the cooperative. The Community Board came out with a demand that the population of the project be 65 percent elderly; and the rest, veterans of all wars. The Forest Hills Residents Association finally announced a plan for eight stories, all for the elderly. All of these plans are aimed at eliminating from the project what are regarded as undesirable tenants—welfare and black poor with children. But if that's done the basic reason for this entire effort is ignored and Forest Hills could prove to be a difficult precedent. If either of these plans (which raise constitutional questions) is adopted, it will become extremely difficult to move low-income families into any middle-class section of our city in the foreseeable future. With some justification, other areas will ask for the same treatment given Forest Hills, and the result will be that the ghetto children may be walled in indefinitely.

I've not taken any public position on the Community Planning Board solution or the Forest Hills Residents Association plan; my Report speaks for itself. I would doubt very much that the mayor could adopt either of them, and I'm positive that Golar would resign before lending his approval or acquiescence.

Now, after all of the weeks of heated debate and the incessant chanting of "No project, no way," it develops that everyone on the opposing side is willing to compromise and the differences are not really large ones. My compromise calls for 12 floors, and now the most distant proposal from the community calls for as many as 8. That's the latest word from the Forest Hills Residents Association, which at the last minute, knowing its position was doomed, decided to jump on the compromise bandwagon. The Forest Hills Residents Association calls for 100 percent elderly, the proposed Cuomo compromise calls for 40 percent of the units elderly. The difference is 60 percent of the units or about 240 apartments, only some 30 of which will eventually be welfare.

From the viewpoint of the ordinary onlooker, what has resulted is a blur of various compromise proposals, indistinct in their particulars but all sharing in common the idea of accommodation and partial relenting. This is all that's needed; it's clear to me that the compromise will work. I'm sure now that if our original plan is adopted, with or without a cooperative, no substantial number will move out, and that was one of the principal objectives.

My guess is that there will be a decision tomorrow, and that despite anything that's said during the hearing the original compromise proposal—with language indicating that it will be made a cooperative if possible—will pass. The mayor has already indicated he will vote for it. Manes will too. Garelik and Beame have no choice because, in the end, their only alternative would be to allow the present three 24's, and neither of them would be willing to do that. They will vote for the compromise reluctantly, blaming the mayor as much as they can. That's 14 votes and all that's needed. Sutton is sure to vote against, as a matter of principle. Abrams should vote against but may not. I can't read Connor and Leone.

Thursday, October 26, 1972

The hearing was held today and I sat through it tempted on several occasions to file my slip. I never did. There was no reason to believe that anything said at the hearing would affect the vote. It was totally predictable. The pro-project people argued in terms of messages and symbols; the anti-project people said what they have been saying for over a year—only this time somewhat muted in tone. Finally, the silent middle ground found a voice: Rosenthal, Koch, Gallent, and Gold all spoke for the compromise. The mayor didn't sit; Deputy Mayor Morrison appeared in his place. The mayor got hell for not being present.

The hearing was the stuff of which great Breslin columns are made. It was ridiculous in places and moving in others. Battista was the first to speak. He excoriated lawyer-planners and told the city to build in the ghetto instead. This received the rousing approval of most of the audience, an audience that consisted of about two hundred anti-project people and twenty or thirty pro. This is the perennial problem with hearings on controversial issues.

Any group sufficiently organized to appear en masse has it within its power to create an atmosphere which is projected by the camera and the reporters present to the city at large. In a very direct way it colors the entire controversy; two hundred rabid anti-project people are able to create a citywide impression that the project is almost universally greeted with disfavor, fear, contempt, and anger. In fact, there is no way of knowing for sure whether that image is accurate. There is no necessary coincidence between the opinion of the people who are able to reach and occupy the Board of Estimate Hall and the sentiment of the community at large. Since, however, it's the only criterion available, it has its impact. It works a strange chemistry on the politicians. Everyone seated at the bench knew that there were hundreds of thousands of potential project tenants who favored the project and who would have—had they been organized—jammed City Hall and the blocks around it causing an entirely different kind of spell. But no one on the board made that point, nor did they—throughout the course of ten hours of hearing—ask more than two or three cogent questions. It was a pathetic charade, as most of these hearings are—the ancient catharsis, a chance for the public to get it off its chest, and they did. Gold was booed and taunted. Apparently none of the thirteen or fourteen thousand people who voted for him had the interest or concern to come to the hearing. Garelik, a symbol of law enforcement, made limp feints and gestures at keeping order. He admonished, cajoled, and threatened, with no effect. He had several opportunities to remove people from the Hall but backed away from them, so that speaker after speaker was greeted with catcalls, shouting, and all the primitive discourtesies and passions that have become characteristic of these hearings. Sutton put on display all of his elegantly smooth, polemical abilities and he dramatically made his pitch for the low-income sector. He was itching for exchanges and was able to involve Joe DeVoy, Herb Miller and several others.

Birbach managed to have himself arrested in the morning, but then Borough President Manes announced to the meeting assembled that he would have Jerry released. Score one for the Community!

An hour later Jerry entered the Hall and was greeted tumultuously with shouts of "We want Jerry," "Our man Jerry," "Give 'em hell, Jerry." He might have been El Cid or Salazar and he enjoyed every minute of it. The middle class was flexing its muscles.

This community knew what counts in these arguments. Speaker after speaker warned the board members that they would remember his vote when their turn to face the populace came. The cleverest of the politician speakers were able to frame their positions with deft lawyerlike ambiguity so that they could sometime later make points with whatever constituency might confront them. No Profiles in Courage would be written on this day.

It went on and on. A scuffle in front, a sit-down at the podium led by Reverend Tim Mitchell. Shouting, crying—all in a room that after a while reeked of perspiration and even foodstuffs that in anticipation of the siege the more prudent and experienced of the battlers had supplied themselves with.

In the back of the room, in a pathetically allegorical incident, a scuffle broke out right next to me between two middle-aged women, one of whom had unceremoniously usurped and bitten the other's—of all things—banana. When the banana owner expressed her dissatisfaction by jamming it into the usurper's face, the fight started. I tried to reconcile the two. Breslin found out about it and concluded, more wisely than humorously, that in the end, perhaps that's what this was all about—a battle over scraps.

It was nearly 9:30 when the vote was taken. The compromise had been approved as submitted except that it was now to be a cooperative, if possible. Manes' demand that it be composed of 65 percent elderly and 35 percent veterans, which was concurred in by most of the board but rejected by Golar and the mayor, was legally ineffective and would not be implemented.

In a well-orchestrated, almost maudlin session the board members ended the night by congratulating themselves profusely, as much as to say that if anything was proven by this ordeal it was their own virtue. The mayor, Manes, Garelik and Beame voted precisely as suspected. Abrams, Leone, and Connor all went with the compromise as well, largely in deference to Manes. Sutton stood fast; they had given him little choice. The mayor, as anticipated, got it from all sides. No one had a kind word for him. No one bothered to mention that at the very least he tried to correct the error. Maybe Napoleon was right: when you make a mistake in government, don't admit it, move on—the masses will never appreciate honesty, they prefer illusions.

While many of the pro-project people talked of a 50 percent sell-out, one could detect some small satisfaction with the "victory" involved. After all, the project would be built, and the 65/35 mix would not be implemented. Time and the jumbled complex of last-minute suggestions and propositions distorted the perspective somewhat, but it was clear just before the hearing that there was still a threat the project might have been killed entirely by a dramatic gesture, however illegal, on the part of the board. The pressure from Birbach and the Queens Jewish Community Council had been great. Surely Beame and Garelik must have considered the potential of a vote which would have dealt the mayor a crushing defeat and won the unlimited admiration of a huge part of the middle-class vote in this town. Many of the pro-project people had expressed this fear throughout the long weeks of discussion. They had mounted their rebuttal, convinced that they could not prevent a reduction but concerned that they might be faced with obliteration of the project. So that to the extent the mayor had stood fast, they had won.

The community too was reluctant to express satisfaction with their achievement, although I'm sure that privately their leaders indicated gratification with the results of their own efforts. At the very least, they had seen the problems created by the proposed development reduced dramatically by the reduction in size. Everyone in the Hall that day had won, and everyone there had lost except those few who truly believed that the reduction was in fact better for all concerned.

One had the feeling that the work would now continue unhampered; the project would be built and that someday all of this would be regarded as somehow vaguely irrelevant. As with Corona, Willets Point, and other similar convulsions in our city's governmental process, the entire situation will be forgotten and whatever lessons might have been learned will be lost to history, a change in ruling powers, and distraction. And there were so many lessons to be learned: the inefficacy and short-sightedness of the housing program, the lack of workable vehicles for community participation, the need for some sort of revamping of the governmental structure, and most of all the glaring, insidious, irrepressible problem of the ghetto. Forest Hills said so much about all of these things—but who will hear it?

Perhaps more than anything else, one who had studied the situation could not help concluding that there had been a lack of common sense manifest throughout. Common sense would have said that before buying a piece of property one ought to determine what the cost of development would be; that before asking a community for its active good will and cooperation with the project one ought to explain to that community the sacrifices involved; that before adopting a policy like the cooperative notion one ought to explore extensively its implications and lay them before the group that is to make the judgment; that a public hearing should be a hearing at which the public is present and at which it is heard before decisions are made. These are simple truths—inescapable ones. One must wonder why they are not seen and acted upon. It can only be because something in our political process—whether it is the necessary allegiances, precommitments to positions, or the existence of political parties—works at cross-purposes with the dictates of reasonableness and common sense. But then this has been true for so long that it seems hardly worth the effort to attempt to change it.

"Hardly worth the effort . . ."—what grim words. I'm sorry I said them. I must be tired. They're bad words—weak, self-pitying, surrender words. It *is* worth the effort; there's no choice but to make the effort. That's what it's all about—it's climbing mountains without ever reaching the top, hoping, despite the slips and slides. That in the long run you're getting closer. And knowing, at least, that you're trying to get closer. It's the trying that counts. And the dull pain of frustration, the quick brief remorse over reversals, that's part of it. And so is the uncertainty—maybe that's the worst of all—not knowing whether you're really making progress, not knowing whether your judgment brought you closer or further from the top. Wondering whether you're right or wrong. That was certainly true here. My compromise has been adopted. That's all that the Board of Estimate resolution has definitely accomplished. But they've added Don Manes' suggestion that it be made a cooperative, "*if possible*." It was imaginative and a good idea—in the abstract. But what if they're not able to work it out legally. Will this provide the community with another occasion for resentment, anger, trouble? Could it start another war? Should I have testified at the board and made these points? Was I right in choosing to remain behind the scenes? Should I have spent more time working on the cooperative notion and put my head to finding legal assurances for it instead of accepting the opinions given by the experts? Could I have done more to move us closer to the top?

I'm afraid the questions will always be there. There will be congratulations, probably a lot of them, but the wondering will still be there.

Friday, October 27, 1972

An interesting coincidence relegated the Forest Hills story to the obscure middle pages this morning. A likely settlement for Vietnam was announced, and in view of it one could not fairly regard the Forest Hills resolution as anything more than incidental. In a way it was probably better that Forest Hills should be permitted to slip into the history books virtually unnoticed.

The mayor called today. The conversation was as crisp and brief as had been the phone call a hundred and sixty-three days ago. The mayor said thank you. I made some clumsy response. Even if I had tried, I couldn't have thought of anything clever. I looked out my window across the bay to New Jersey for a long time—trying to feel something.

Epilogue

Shortly after the Board of Estimate hearing on October 26, 1972, the first steel framework began to show above the foundations of the three apartment buildings. The steel moved upward gradually but irrepressibly, floor after floor. Then, at the top of the twelfth floor it stopped abruptly and was capped by the roof beams. By November of 1973 it was clear that the compromise had stuck: there would be three 12-story apartment houses occupied by 432 low-income families, and not the 24-story towers originally proposed.

But some confusion still surrounded Borough President Manes' proposal to convert the project into a cooperative. Although he had worked with the federal authorities for months and almost everyone agreed it was a good and innovative idea, there remained some doubt as to whether the plan was legal and would become a working reality. And even if it did, it was uncertain to what extent the board of directors of the cooperative, appointed by the borough president, would be able to control or screen tenants.

Several weeks of quiet had followed the adoption of the compromise by the Board of Estimate. Everyone involved was spent and the holidays provided a convenient respite. When signs of a revived interest appeared in the beginning of 1973, they were spotty and relatively disorganized.

A week after the board's action, Simeon Golar had announced his intention to ask for an increase in the amount of income that could be earned by a family while still qualifying as low-income tenants. The effect unmistakably was to increase the number of near-middle-class tenants in housing projects and to reduce proportionately the percentage of welfare tenants. This was a clear concession to many arguments that had been urged by the community throughout the Forest Hills struggle. But the statement appeared and disappeared in the local newspapers almost unnoticed, with no gloating and no "I told you so"s.

During the ensuing weeks, voices here and there from Forest Hills demanded assurance of the cooperative and a definitive statement as to what was going on. But none of these voices rose to anywhere near the pre-compromise pitch. Occasionally a small knot of the Forest Hills residents joined together in protest rallies insisting that it was not too late to stop the project entirely and to convert it into a residence for senior citizens exclusively, but they were hardly noticed. Threats of further lawsuits were uttered, but they had become tiresome.

The old fire was gone. The army had been disbanded and the general had left the field. Jerry Birbach went on a diet, lost thirty pounds, and with it much of his old image. He moved out of Forest Hills and into Holliswood in Queens, a few miles away. But he did so quietly and with barely any impact on the community he left behind. The rumors were that Jerry had struck up an alliance with the establishment politicians in Queens and was preparing to pursue a new political career. He had little to say about Forest Hills.

The 1973 mayoralty election dominated the news. John Lindsay's announcement that he would not seek a third term opened the field wide, and a dozen or so candidates plunged in. In July of 1973 Abraham Beame and Herman Badillo, a Jew and a Puerto Rican, met in the first run-off election in the history of the city's mayoralty. Beame won decisively and became the odds-on favorite to defeat three other candidates in the general election.

Throughout the ceaseless rhetoric of the primaries and the mayoral campaign, scatter-site housing was not an important issue. The positions of the candidates had apparently become homogenized. The popular liberal phrases that had predominated only a few years earlier had been filed away for use at a more propitious time. None of the candidates argued for integration or dispersal of ghetto residents in middle-class areas. The new and safer emphasis was on rehabilitating the ghettos. The clock had been turned back nearly two decades, and many people felt that the impetus for this withdrawal had been provided by Forest Hills.

Nationally, the position on housing for the poor changed even more dramatically. President Nixon announced a new housing policy in late September of 1973. The new policy—if indeed it could be called that—seemed to many a grim surrender to the enormous complexities of the problem. In effect it concluded that the federal government had no real answer. Instead of formulating vehicles to provide decent housing for the poor in areas outside of ghetto concentration and free from the oppressive effects of those environments, the Nixon policy was to be, for the most part, a simple doling out of cash subsidies directly to the needy, leaving them to their own devices to find suitable housing. Many of those experienced in the situation pointed out sadly that the policy was nothing but a cop-out which would in all likelihood result in a massive underwriting of slumlords. A former governor of Pennsylvania noted that federal money would now be used to house low-income tenants in chicken coops, thus enriching exploiters, further depressing the needy, and abusing the federal treasury.

At least one federal official stated that Forest Hills had been a significant factor in inducing the new federal program. And after all is said and done, that may prove to be the real tragedy of the Forest Hills experience: that it will not be a producer, but a destroyer; that it will not teach, but will only intimidate; that in the end, it will have helped to kill an imperfect program and create a worse one.

It was as a small attempt to salvage something from the anguish and frustration of Forest Hills that I agreed—not without reservations—to permit the diary to be published. I was reluctant because

I had put down these notes privately and without considering the possible judgments of others who might read my words but not understand my thoughts because they had been so imperfectly transmitted to paper. I also knew that the record was chronologically and factually incomplete. It started at a time long after important forces had already come into play, and it failed to record—because I did not know them at the time—many contemporaneous events that were significant. Thus, it was only after the diary notes closed that I learned the full dimensions of the behind-the-scenes activities of Borough President Manes and Mayor Lindsay, who worked doggedly throughout the compromise effort in an attempt to reconcile the warring factions. Nor did I tell of the work of Dave Starr, editor of the *Long Island Press*, who, as a mutual friend and adviser to both the borough president and the mayor, spent long hours thinking, talking, and working toward the single end of a reasonable and peaceful accommodation. There are other events and actions of people not recorded because they were then not known.

Nevertheless, I agreed to publish this limited description of the significant events, forces, people, and philosophies that made the conflict in Forest Hills in the hope that—instead of being submerged in the flood of greater and more momentous events—the Forest Hills experience might survive long enough to teach us something about our system and ourselves. In fact, I believe there is much to learn from this significant episode in the history of urban government. Forest Hills tells us a great deal about the true feelings of the people actually involved on both sides of the issues. It points up the huge gap between abstract sociological propositions and their efficacy—or lack of it—when nailed down to the Procrustean bed of urban reality. It shows up dramatically the difficulty of attempting to sell by means of homily—and the brandishing of moral obligations—social cures that require sacrifice by some for the good of others. It shows, painfully, the need for more effective devices of communication between centralized urban government and the communities affected by governmental projects. And it reminds us that one of the serious impediments to the resolution of complex confrontations is the tendency of the parties to maintain fixed and extreme positions, the lack of subtlety in dialogue and argumentation, the loss of reasonableness. It seems to me that here, as in most similar situations, the only safe route past Scylla and Charybdis is somewhere between them. What's needed is a sturdy ship and a sound navigator. In the end, any description of the Forest Hills experience will inevitably raise more questions than it answers and will necessarily be in part depressing and in part hopeful. But then, that will always be true: there will always be more problems than solutions; more to be done than has been done; more quests than conquests. The game is lost only when we stop trying.

Appendix

REPORT TO HONORABLE JOHN V. LINDSAY CONCERNING
THE PROPOSED LOW-INCOME HOUSING PROJECT
AT 108th STREET, FOREST HILLS, QUEENS

INTRODUCTORY NOTE

On May 17th of this year you asked me "to make an independent exploration of possible revisions in the Forest Hills housing project and the overall planning for low-income housing in Queens and to make recommendations to the Mayor, the City Council and the Board of Estimate for any changes." Specifically, you requested that I explore the question "with key City officials, especially members of the City Planning Commission and Housing Authority, members of the Board of Estimate and City Council, with Federal and State legislators and housing officials, and representatives of community groups and private agencies." Beyond these directions you in no way limited or qualified the steps I was to take. In point of fact you asked that I take the assignment with a completely open mind and "freedom to make any recommendations [I] think appropriate." I have spent the past nine weeks attempting to comply with these directions and I offer you, the Board of Estimate and the City Council this report of my investigation and conclusions.

THE INVESTIGATION

The investigative process involved three major phases. The first required a research into the basic legal and factual context. This involved a study of the controlling Federal and City statutes and ordinances, the applicable administrative law, including the H.U.D. guidelines and Housing Authority regulations, and the most recent constitutional law concerning limitations upon the use of Federal housing funds.

My study of the physical facts and the administrative genesis and history of the project began with an investigation of the original so-called scatter site program that was sought to be implemented by your administration beginning early in 1966. In so far as it was possible, I explored the proposal for Corona, the moving of the project from Corona to 108th Street, the hearings before the City Planning Commission and the Board of Estimate, and the somewhat obscure history of the intervening period from 1967 to 1971. Since the activity in this later period consisted mostly of work on the physical plans for the project and various negotiations with Federal officials, my sources of information were basically the recollections and opinions of individuals involved during that period. I have reviewed everything that has occurred since 1971 by reading various newspaper accounts and by discussions with numerous City officials. The actual physical details of the project itself are, of course, clearly set out in the architectural plans. Additionally, the studies by the Comptroller General and the finely detailed Environmental Statement prepared by H.U.D. provided full descriptions of the physical situation. I was further aided in this regard by the generous assistance of a number of volunteer professionals—lawyers, architects, real estate appraisers, builders and planners—who freely gave me the benefit of their knowledge and expertise.

A second aspect of the investigative procedure consisted of discussions with various groups, community and religious leaders and ordinary citizens who wished to express a point of view. Since it was clear to me from the outset that there were literally thousands of individuals and groups who wished to participate, I decided against selecting among them. Instead, I made myself available to any individuals and groups who wished to be heard and were willing to make an appointment. The alternative would have been to pick and choose at the risk of being imperfectly eclectic thereby depriving some of a fair opportunity to be heard. In this connection Boro President Manes helped by making available a large conference room in the Queens County Boro Hall building. The room was put to good use; it was utilized every weekday night except Friday for a few weeks, and it enabled me to hear the opinions of at least a few hundred individuals and groups. While these meetings were for the most part arranged by appointment at the request of the people who wished to be heard, there were times when citizens and groups appeared without prior notice. They were all heard after the regularly scheduled appointments and in no case was anyone turned away, notwithstanding this required on a number of occasions that the building be used until well past midnight.

My availability for discussion at Boro Hall was well publicized in all branches of the media and the end result was that I had the benefit of an extensive exposure to the sentiments, fears and aspirations of the community at large. I spoke with a large number of homeowners, project tenants and professional planners, both black and white. More than a hundred Forest Hills Residents Association members appeared individually and gave me their views. They were remarkably uniform in their presentations. I had a number of discussions with this organization's President, including a three hour meeting shortly before the conclusion of my investigation. Many groups and individuals who disagreed categorically with the position presented by the Residents Association were heard as well. My discussions also included long talks and exchanges of views with the Community Board Chairman of each of three Boards that cover the area in which the site is located and the neighborhood immediately around it. Hundreds of communications—letters, briefs and position papers—were received. Every one was read and its contents considered.

Literally dozens of elected officials offered their advice and recommendations. Others had presented their views in papers which I studied. Chairman Golar of the Housing Authority and a number of his deputies cooperated in supplying facts and offering points of view. Two of his staff took the time to conduct me on a tour of housing projects throughout the City. Members (present and past) of the Department of City Planning and the Planning Commission gave their views and opinions. H.U.D. officials, including Regional Administrator William S. Green, Area Director John Maylott and Assistant Director for Technical Service Leo Haberman were extraordinarily helpful. Police Commissioner Murphy and a number of police officers of the 112th Precinct in Forest Hills also took time to discuss the situation.

In addition to all of the above, dozens of other individuals came forward as volunteers to participate in this investigation. Retired upper-echelon police officials, professional planners from outside the City of New York, former students of mine at St. John's Law School and other well intentioned private citizens contacted me to offer whatever assistance they could.

The final phase of this process was my analysis and the conclusions which are hereinafter summarized.

Whether or not this report helps to produce a workable solution in Forest Hills it will nevertheless be true that this undertaking itself has been, in my judgment, an excellent demonstration of the intelligent and generous concern of which this City is capable. With insignificant exceptions, my efforts were greeted with excellent cooperation by people whose only motive was simply to help resolve a difficult problem. Many of these individuals, for their own reasons, asked that their participation be kept anonymous. I have agreed to do so. With that reservation I would like you to know that I have kept a careful daily account of everything that has been done in the course of this investigation and that account, which now exceeds 200 typewritten pages, will be available to you as a supplement to these comments. It describes in much greater detail than is feasible in the report the various components of personalities and ideas which were integral parts of this judgment-making process.

THE PROPOSED PROJECT: A CRITICISM OF ITS SIZE

The Scatter Site Requirement

The proposed project must be measured against the purposes it was designed to serve. The so called "scatter site" concept was essentially intended to break the cruel and self-destructive cycle of poverty in ghetto areas. The dimension of the poverty problem and the need for housing are enormous. One would have to be blind, cruel or both not to use these realities as starting points in any consideration of this problem. Scatter site projects were designed to help low-income people by moving them out of ghetto areas and into middle income neighborhoods. The hoped-for improvement was obviously not merely physical in nature; that could be accomplished simply by replacing deteriorated ghetto buildings with new structures. Rather they were intended to produce an upward mobility or opportunity for social uplift by encouraging assimilation of the low income population into a new and "better" environment. This, roughly speaking, is the sociological predicate for the concept.

There is another aspect to the principle which arises out of the constitutional implications of housing people through the use of Federal funds in ghetto areas. In recent years and ever since *Brown* v. *Board of Education* it has become increasingly clear that any use of Federal funds which results directly or indirectly, intentionally or inadvertently, in a pattern of segregation will be struck down by the courts. The City's housing program depends largely upon Federal funds. The vast majority of people who have been lifted out of ghetto hovels and placed in newer and more civilized structures owe these new facilities ultimately to the Federal subsidies which permitted them to be built. Without these funds the present housing crisis would become a housing calamity. That possibility is so grotesque that until recently it was apparently not seriously considered. By virtue of a number of recent court decisions, however, the prospect has become not only a real, but a critical one. The law is now predictably clear that if Federal housing funds are used exclusively in racially concentrated areas, like the ghettos of New York City, and are not used, in respectable part, to move non-white low-income people into non-racially concentrated areas, the Federal government would be required to cut off *all* housing funds for whatever purpose. Translated into the realities of New York City, this rule of law means that unless this City uses Federal funds to move significant numbers of non-white low-income people into white communities (almost necessarily middle class), the entire housing program could be jeopardized.

Some of the opponents of the project argue that this application of constitutional principle is unwise, but it is a reality concerning which this City has little choice. Indeed, in addition to the constitutional mandate, the principle is now enjoined upon the City by the H.U.D. administrative guidelines. The City must, therefore, either honor the principle or risk real disaster.

As I understand the law, the constitutional rule does not require that low income people be moved into middle income areas *en masse;* theoretically, the Section 23 sub-leasing program which places low income people in privately owned buildings could accomplish compliance. But there is a practical problem with this approach. To begin with, mere tokenism will not satisfy the constitutional requirements; the numbers of people placed outside the areas of racial concentration must be significant when measured against the entire number of people housed in ghetto projects or the ostensible compliance would necessarily have to be disregarded as sham. Under present conditions, both because of the ceilings fixed by Federal law and, more importantly, because of the private sector's reluctance to make apartments available in middle income areas, it has not been possible to move sufficiently large numbers of low income people into middle income communities through the use of this program. According to H.U.D. figures, there are fewer than four thousand units presently leased through Section 23 and most of those in Queens County are located in racially concentrated areas.

The Section 23 program seems to me—and, more importantly to many experts in the field—a more intelligent *theoretical* approach to scatter site planning. But theory is not enough; until this program can be moved out of the conceptual stage and into the state of full practical realization, it would be nothing but cynicism, or worse, to suggest it as a complete alternative to project housing.

In short, it appears that this City is presently required to build low-income housing for significant numbers of people in middle income areas. Whether the building of these projects as part of the so called scatter site program is regarded as a response to a sociological principle or a legal obligation, its effectiveness in terms of improving the lot of the people who are being housed depends necessarily on the survival of a middle class environment and upon the receptivity, or at least lack of hostility, on the part of the middle class community. Clearly, if in fact the entry upon the scene of the project were to result in a resistance and hostility that eventually produced a change in the character of the community so that it became a racially concentrated low-income area, the scatter site project would be self-destructive.

The History of the Project

Before 1966 when this City attempted to implement the scatter site approach, there had been relatively little in-depth study and analysis of the program's potential effectiveness. The program was largely an enthusiastic experiment in social planning. Its goals were noble but its efficacy largely unproven. I believe events have now shown that the City tried to do too much too fast in Forest Hills. In retrospect it now seems clear that it would have been better to move cautiously and only after the fullest possible discussion with the community. That did not occur.

There is reason to believe that the original allocation of units was determined more by the necessity of meeting a minimum number of city-wide units mandated by Federal regulation than by a calculated judgment as to the number of units that could be profitably borne by the area selected. When the project was first conceived, it was intended for Corona and then it would have contained only 509 units. The project as so designed was aborted almost immediately after conception and the site was changed (for reasons that have never been fully and clearly understood by the public) to 108th Street. The fact that it was vacant and undeveloped was apparently regarded as the new site's principal advantage. It should have been apparent that the nature of the subsoil conditions was such that the cost of development would be extraordinarily high. But that appears to have caused little concern. In fact, this hard economic fact eventually created a Procrustean bed over which the entire design, and consequently the size of the project, had to be twisted and tortured. The judgment that the project had to consist of as many as 840 units was not arrived at as a matter of desirability; it was rather the result produced by the cost of acquiring and curing the land, coupled with the strictures of the Federal guidelines.

It is true, of course, that despite these difficulties, the project was approved by a unanimous Board of Estimate following public hearing in December of 1966. The Courts have affirmed that the hearing satisfied the broad legal parameters but as one who has been close to the hearing process in this City for the last ten years, it is clear to me that neither the Board of Estimate nor the City at large had the benefit of the community's true point of view. The hearing system operated as it was designed to but that system was—and is—intrinsically faulty. Very little had been done preceding the hearing to inform the community as to the details and precise implications of the proposal. The Community Planning Board learned of the hearing and proposal by accident and too late to reach and involve significant numbers of residents. The Board's decision was made late on a Friday afternoon when a large segment of the opposition, Orthodox Jews who were residents in the area, were forbidden by their religious commitment to be present and participate. As a result, despite the good intentions of the members of the Board who sat, it is unrealistic to say that the hearings were truly reflective of the community's view. History has shown this to be so.

After that hearing, three years of apparent inactivity permitted the community to be lulled into a false conclusion that the project would never be built, so that when it was finally announced that work would proceed at the site, what was heard from the community was actually the first true indication of its sentiments. It expressed those sentiments very clearly—so clearly that it is reasonable to suspect if their position had been stated as forcefully at the outset, the project would never have been approved as presently planned. Indeed, many of those who have spoken out strenuously against any suggestion of compromise stated concern that any return of the project to the Board of Estimate now, would inevitably result in a rejection of the entire plan.

These brief references to the history of the project and the failure of the system to produce a meaningful communication with the affected community would be pointless if they were intended purely as criticism—they are not. They should assist in the understanding of the community position today and serve as an aid in the planning of future housing projects.

When the community was belatedly heard, it made a number of

arguments which were plausible even if not decisive. The arguments with respect to congestion, the concomitant strain on community services and facilities and the violation of scale could hardly be called fatuous. One may concede that any large placement of additional residents almost anywhere in this City would be greeted with similar arguments. The pervasiveness of the complaint, however, hardly appears to be reason for ignoring it entirely.

These irritations and the unfortunate earlier history combined together to exacerbate what I would regard as the principal problem, and that is the concern of many in the community that the placing of 840 low-income units in their midst would bring as its inevitable concomitant increasing crime, vandalism, exodus and deterioration. This fear, in turn, has created hostility.

Not everybody in the Forest Hills community is hostile to the project as presently planned but in different degrees a substantial number of the residents in the area are either fearful or seriously concerned. The degrees of fear and hostility can be measured almost precisely in concentric circles radiating out from the middle of the site. Those in the closest circle geographically are the most fearful. As the bands formed by these circles become more remote from the actual site, the degree of concern diminishes until ultimately, when sufficiently removed geographically, the predominant opinion becomes more "liberal" and tolerant.

The attitude of the community immediately affected must be given serious consideration. In my judgment it exists in substantial enough degree and in large enough numbers of people so that it might eventually lead to large scale departures. I sought to resist this conclusion at the outset of my investigation and regarded the evidence offered me skeptically. But now, at the conclusion of my study and after hundreds of hours of discussion, formal and informal with scores of Forest Hills residents, I am persuaded that unless this fear is in some manner mitigated, the possibility that the project will be jeopardized by large numbers of people leaving Forest Hills is a real one. I am also persuaded that attitude can be substantially changed if not totally dissipated.

Whether or not one regards such an attitude as morally defensible or even reasonable, might be considered beside the point. Unless altered, this attitude might eventually nullify whatever good is sought to be achieved by the project. If, in fact, large numbers of surrounding apartment dwellers were to relocate, they would in all likelihood not be replaced by other middle income residents. It is reasonable to assume that with the drying up of that market, landlords would turn to the rent supplement and welfare sector. Depending upon the rate of departure (and experience indicates that the momentum accelerates), the City might, before long, be faced with a bizarre irony; it would then have created by the project precisely what it sought to avoid, another racially concentrated low income community, and the net result would have been to spread the ghetto instead of containing it. This result would be a misfortune for the project tenants—its implications with respect to the housing policy, even nationwide, are worse. It is now almost trite to observe that Forest Hills has become a focus of attention nationally. What happens here will inevitably be regarded as a lesson for cities elsewhere. Therefore, a sense of obligation to the needy who are served by the national housing policy, as well as self-concern, require that this City bend every effort to make Forest Hills work, and this requires, in turn, that community responsiveness and cooperation be somehow encouraged.

By placing the emphasis upon the reality of the hostility in the Forest Hills community without respect to its justification or lack thereof, I do not mean to suggest that I regard that concern as utterly baseless. Certainly the perfidious generalization that all low income, or for that matter welfare, people are vandals and criminals would be universally rejected by reasonable men. On the other hand, to deny that poverty and social problems are related would be to deny the testimony of history and our own experience in this City. Where there are large concentrations of impoverished people there are normally large concentrations of social problems. This is, effectively, part of the rationale for the scatter site principle itself, which starts with the proposition that poor people ought to be removed from large concentrations of poor people precisely because those areas are particularly infected by social problems. One need only to travel through this City to confirm the deterioration that has been occasioned by the spread of poverty areas. This hard experience is fresh in the minds of many of the Forest Hills residents who fled from that kind of erosion in Brooklyn, The Bronx and Manhattan into Forest Hills where, by dint of their own efforts and the benediction of the fates, they have been able to create a community and a life style relatively free from the kinds of problems that oppress the ghetto dweller.

If the concern of the Forest Hills community with the project as now planned, and the erosion of the present character of that community which it threatens, could be allayed by intelligent disputation, that would have occurred already. The Chairman of the Housing Authority has made many persistent and articulate attempts to defend the project in its present dimensions. He has appeared publicly, debated, argued, and cajoled, all to no avail. One must conclude that if the community is not now convinced that a project of 840 units is workable, it never will be.

Part of the difficulty with the Chairman's attempts to persuade the opponents of the project that their fears were ill-founded arose from the references to tenant selection. In various ways and at various times it was suggested to the people of Forest Hills that tenants for the project would be carefully screened. While there is no doubt in my mind that Chairman Golar, whose reputation for integrity and competence has survived the most bitter assaults, fully intends to do everything possible to weed out potential "troublemakers," the fact is that he has only a limited legal and practical ability to do so. The Forest Hills community is aware of this and therefore the effect of the declaration was merely to underscore that there may be potential problem tenants, without supplying assurance that they will be screened out.

The Project As Planned Is Too Large

Even prescinding from the attitude of the Forest Hills community, it seems to me that objectively viewed the project as proposed is simply too large, both in terms of its physical size and in the number of low-income units it will add to the community.

For whatever it is worth, (and given the difficulty of finding hard standards of measurement it may be worth a great deal) the fact is that there has been, publicly recorded, a large body of responsible opinion condemning the size of the project. Planners, commentators, and all of the elected public officials in the area have spoken out against the dimensions of the project as presently planned. In so doing they make a number of points. They note that 840 units comprising a new population of perhaps three thousand people, many of them children, will severely tax the present transportation and school facilities. A scrutiny of the Environmental Statement and the Comptroller General's studies indicate to me that these objections were never substantially refuted; rather, the points appear to have been accepted as made and the community told that it should be consoled by the prospect that transportation and school facilities would be developed within the next several years to meet the need. One should not be surprised at the skepticism of a community which is asked to wait an indeterminate number of years for relief from problems about which they have complained for decades.

The physical size of the buildings has been repeatedly condemned. They are, indeed, out of scale with the immediately surrounding buildings and it seems to me not a persuasive answer to point to other buildings in the general vicinity which are regarded with equal distaste and repugnance. As you know, for the past year the Forest Hills and Kew Gardens communities have mounted a vigorous attack against the plans of a private builder to develop *luxury* high risers of twenty floors only about a mile from the 108th Street site.

The H.U.D. guidelines, and the almost unanimous opinion of professional planners, all show a dissatisfaction with high rise structures for projects of this sort. They are concededly to be discouraged where elderly tenants are concerned. A professional architect who had made a careful study of the problem of housing for the elderly submitted a thesis demonstrating support for her proposition that high rise buildings had a debilitating and depressing effect on elderly tenants. They are also generally regarded as undesirable for family units. The Federal Court in the *Gautreaux* case specifically condemned high risers for scatter site planning. The Court went as far as to suggest an arbitrary limit on the number of floors and units in a "proper" scatter site project. While such maxima would have to be employed with great caution since they are obviously dependent upon the precise statistical, physical and demographic characteristics of the area involved, they clearly describe an attitude which would regard the Forest Hills project as presently proposed to be egregiously large.

I have heard from a number of experts in law enforcement and crime prevention who state flatly that from a security point of view these three twenty-four story towers are at best undesirable.

An obvious difficulty created by the size of the proposed project, particularly when taken with the scale of the buildings, is that it threatens to create a development so large and so obviously distinct from the surrounding community that it will have the effect of self-containment. This, of course, would operate counter to the objective of scatter site housing, which is to permit a meld of the tenants into the surrounding community. As presently planned, this project is large enough to create a community of its own so that in the end, even if the surrounding area were not to change, the City might simply have transplanted a substantial segment of the ghetto into another geographical area.

It appears to be self-evident that the larger and more visible the project, the greater the discouragement of assimilation. While Pruitt-Igoe in St. Louis and Queensbridge in Queens County are much larger than the proposed project, and may be otherwise distinguishable, I regard them as support for the general proposition that as the size is increased, the chance for accomplishing the objectives of scatter site housing is diminished.

Of great significance is the fact that the principal rationale in *favor* of the present size is the economic necessity created by the choice of land. I have noted that on the original Corona site, where the City was not burdened by the same land problem, the City's judgment was that 509 units would have been sufficient for the project. The size has been not so much argued for as it has been excused on the theory that it was compelled by the cost factors. These are obviously real factors. The Federal guidelines are major constraints on good planning theory. But given that reality one may nevertheless conclude, as I have, that the great danger inherent in the size is not worth the savings.

VARIOUS PROPOSED REVISIONS AND MY RECOMMENDATIONS

Various Proposals

In the course of this investigation I have listened to and argued dozens of viewpoints. Where revisions were suggested they dealt basically with two types of reduction; one purely physical, the other a reduction of the number of low-income family units. It is, of course, necessarily true that if the physical size is reduced the number of units will be reduced. On the other hand, some have emphasized a reduction in low-income family units even irrespective of a change in size.

Any reduction of the size of the building beneath twenty stories will probably require a contribution by the City. I have spent a good deal of time with the H.U.D. officials, and particularly with Mr. Leo Haberman, in an attempt to project the probable costs resultant upon various reductions in the size of the project. These have also been discussed with the architect Mr. Samuel Paul. A complete cost analysis prepared by Mr. Haberman is attached to this report as "Addendum A." It provides figures for assumed reductions in stages of two floors, down to twelve floors. Please keep in mind that the figures he sets forth are estimates which while accurate enough to be usable for present purposes may vary somewhat with the change of factors such as the results of renegotiation with the contractor and the cost of re-design.

A word should be said on these factors. Depending upon the size of the reduction the cost per dwelling unit would be altered. When that cost exceeds the Federal guidelines, the amount of the excess would have to be made up by the City unless the guidelines were to be waived. (That is shown on Addendum A as "Equity Contribution.") (I have no reason to believe that these guidelines would be waived, although I would certainly not discourage an attempt to do so.) It should also be considered, however, that if the buildings were to be reduced, the cost of construction would also be reduced. The reduction in the amount of the cost of construction cannot be precisely measured now and will depend upon negotiations with the contractor, although there is certain to be an overall reduction in the amount of Federal funds needed for the project. (The estimated difference in construction costs for each assumed reduction in height is available on the Addendum.)

It is also worth noting that a change in the size of the buildings might affect the present drainage situation. As now proposed, storm drainage would be removed from the site by pumping. If the number of floors in the building are substantially reduced, the load on the soil might be sufficiently diminished so that the design with respect to drainage could be improved. If the site grade and entrances to the buildings could be raised to the level of the surrounding streets, the drainage system could conceivably be changed to a less costly gravity system. While such a change would require the addition of fill, it is reasonable to believe that the cost of the fill would not far exceed the cost of the gravity system and the net result would be a more efficient design.

A reduction of the building would require re-designing but if the configuration of the buildings were permitted to remain as now planned, the piling at the site could be utilized. Assuming that the piling was sufficient to carry the load of the presently planned three twenty-four story towers it would of course follow that the same piling for lower buildings would amount to an over-design. At least, however, that would quash the lingering skepticism on the part of many concerning the ability of the piling to carry the presently proposed structures.

In considering reduction of the buildings, I have also looked into the possibility of eliminating one of the buildings entirely as an alternative to, or in combination with, the reduction of the size of the other buildings. Figures for that alternative are also set forth on Addendum A.

If the city were to decide to reduce the buildings or in any other way to change the design, then the first step—and it should be taken immediately —would be to call in the contractors and architect for consultation and negotiations. I have spoken with the architect on several occasions and I have also been in touch with Counsel for P. J. Carlin Company. They have been told generally about the possibility of a reduction in the buildings; they would be willing to sit down with the City as soon as requested. My impression is that both would do everything possible to cooperate.

For your information, there follows a brief outline of some of the positions urged upon me:

1. Some of those with whom I spoke took the position that the project as presently proposed should remain intact. Their feeling is that this is particularly so if the City will have to pay to reduce the size of the project. The argument was predicted principally upon the obvious need for low-income housing. Some of these saw the issue as essentially a moral and "symbolic" one. They argued that the principles of scatter site and integration were at stake. Many, as previously noted, appeared to oppose a compromise not so much because they objected to a reduction in the size, but rather because they feared that the ostensible compromise would result in an undoing of the project entirely at the Board of Estimate.

2. A substantial number of the Forest Hills Residents Association took the position that there should be no project at all at 108th Street no matter what financial cost to the City this would entail. They argued essentially against the principle of scatter site itself. Most of these were either unaware of the constitutional requirement, unable to understand it when it was suggested to them, or simply unwilling to accept the proposition that this law must be complied with. Some suggested that this project be halted and an intensive attempt be made to have the Supreme Court of the United States reverse the law as it now is. A number of these opponents offered alternatives to the housing project including: a parking garage, veteran's hospital, public school, state or city office building and other similar improvements. The premise of all these alternatives was, of course, that no low income housing units be placed on the site.

3. The officers of the Forest Hills Residents Association stated that they would consider garden apartments for the elderly low income as a suitable compromise. The selection of elderly low-income was obviously intended to avoid what this group regards as the problems inherent in low income families with children, such as the strain on school and transportation facilities and the danger of vandalism and crime. The limitation to what they regard as a relatively innocuous population was joined with the request for a huge reduction in the size of the buildings principally because they seek assurance that units which might initially be given over to the elderly will not eventually become occupied by families: obviously, the best way to guarantee that is simply to limit the number of physical units. These leaders also suggested that scatter site be accomplished through means of the rent supplement program. I have already noted that I would personally regard that method of dispersal as theoretically superior to the building of institutional housing but that at the present time it is simply unrealistic to believe that a sufficiently significant number of families could be housed through this device. To accept this position, therefore, would be

to violate the moral obligation to low-income people in need of housing and to risk a legal restriction against the use of housing funds anywhere.

4. Between the two extreme positions there were a large variety of intermediate suggestions involving various combinations of size and composition. By far, most of the suggestions were in this area. There are an almost infinite number of permutations possible; many of them were offered. Thus, in some cases it was suggested that the buildings be left intact physically but be used exclusively for the elderly. A number of others recommended no reduction but that the mix be altered by selling off a portion of the site for Mitchell Lama, Section 236 or both. Some suggested a project that would be turned over to Mitchell Lama in its entirety with an agreement to give back a certain percentage of units (e.g. 40%, 30%, 20%) for low income. Others called for a $\frac{1}{3}$, $\frac{1}{3}$, $\frac{1}{3}$ mix which would have produced 280 units of middle income, 280 units elderly low-income and 280 low-income family. These numbers change with changes in the size of the buildings so that, by way of illustration, a $\frac{1}{3}$ formula, given a reduction to 18 stories, would mean approximately 216 units of middle income, 216 elderly low-income and 216 family low-income.

The mix approach is consistent with the scatter site concept and if done internally to the project itself, by placing middle income and low in the same buildings, it creates at least theoretically a submerging of the low-income tenant in the middle income environment. Psychologically, this method of assimilation could reduce the stigmatic disadvantages of straight low-income projects. These advantages are more evident in the case where a mix is internal to the building; if separate buildings were used for the separate component groups there would be a consequent clearer identification and reduced merging. My investigation further disclosed that there is a shortage of 236 money at present. An intensive effort by the City and Federal authorities might, however, be able to produce the Federal funds needed.

Recommendations: Reduction in Size and Number of Units

Overall, it is my opinion that the revision in the project should attempt to reduce the number of dwelling units to an acceptable level and should devote them entirely for low-income housing purposes. I regard the acceptable level as being approximately 430 units (actually 432) in three buildings each 12 stories high.

The suggestion that the buildings be reduced to 12 stories and the units of low-income housing to 432 best stands the test of the available criteria:

1. A reduction to 12 stories will put the scale of this project beneath that of the adjoining Fairview Apartments and closer to a tolerable level although still higher than other neighboring buildings.

2. Given the scarcity of talismanic criteria of judgment in trying to determine the wisest number of units, the availability of Latimer Gardens as a precedent is particularly helpful. It is only a few miles from 108th Street in Flushing and it has been pointed to by the Chairman of the Housing Authority as a good illustration of how well scatter site housing can work. I agree completely with the Chairman's appraisal. While dissidents may argue that Latimer Gardens is in its first wave of tenacies and may change within the next few years, the present reality is to me a more reliable factor than the objectors' speculations.

—The number of units at Latimer Gardens is 423:

—The buildings there are 10 floors high;

—The population is approximately the same as that projected for the Forest Hills project as reduced;

—The percentage of elderly in the Forest Hills project would be approximately 5% higher than at Latimer Gardens.

3. At 432 units the project as here recommended would be approximately 85% of the size of this project when it was originally designed for Corona.

4. As reduced, the project in my opinion would be sufficiently significant in size to obviate the charge of tokenism with respect to compliance with the Federal constitutional principles.

5. Even as reduced the project would honor the scatter site concept and the principle of integration and would thereby maintain its "symbolic" significance.

Although there are certain to be some who will contend that even 432 units are too many, I would not recommend a reduction beyond that point. Anything less will move too close to dangerous ground so far as constitutional implication is concerned and would not fairly reflect the enormity of the need for low income housing. Nor can I find any substantial reason to regard the Forest Hills community as less able to absorb a project of this size than is the Flushing community in which Latimer Gardens is located. Finally, I have been informed that the cost to the City consequent upon a reduction to 12 floors would be the maximum fiscally feasible for the City—assuming it was willing. It must be kept in mind that until a few months ago it would have been, as a practical matter, fiscally impossible for the City to finance any substantial reduction. I was aware of this at the time of my appointment and for obvious reasons regarded it as a matter of first priority in my investigation. I discussed the problem with the former Budget Director, now Deputy Mayor, Mr. Hamilton, and was told that recent changes by the State in the tax equalization rate and the effect of those changes on the debt limit have altered the fiscal picture so that it would now be possible to finance the amounts needed for the revisions I suggest. This, of course, assumes that all necessary approvals could be received. I should add that Mr. Hamilton took no position as to the desirability of the expenditures or a possible change in the project, and was firm in telling me that the amounts in question would constitute an outer limit.

According to the H.U.D. estimate (Addendum A) the reduction to 12 stories would require the City to make an equity contribution of approximately $2,400,000 assuming that the H.U.D. guidelines could not be further waived. The H.U.D. figures also indicate, however, that the net reduction in construction costs would be nearly $8,000,000. Even assuming that the contractor were able to show that the projected decrease in construction costs is too generous, it is still reasonable to expect that there will be a difference of several millions of dollars in the cost of construction. As a technical matter this money would then be subtracted from the Annual Contributions Contract between the City and the Federal government. But it would appear to me entirely possible that the Federal government might agree to reallocate the surplus to other projects or programs so that in effect this money would be available to the City for additional housing.

There are sure to be those who despite this will say the cost to the City consequent upon this change is intolerable. I disagree. I see it as the necessary price for assuring the project's success. The amount at stake is nearly incalculable; the investment is a good one.

If this suggestion (or for that matter any proposal to reduce the buildings substantially) were to be adopted, I would recommend, as already noted, that the City call in the architect and contractors immediately. Since piling has not been completed and the next stage is capping, it is possible that if steps were taken immediately to commence re-designing, the contractors' work could be progressed without interruption while the new design was being prepared.

The reduction here proposed and, indeed, any substantial reduction in the number and size of units should be passed upon by the Board of Estimate. While it is not entirely clear to me from a reading of the Court of Appeals opinion in the *Margulis* case, at precisely what point re-submission to the Board is legally required, I would recommend that the prudent course would be to re-submit in this case. More than that, since any compromise would depend for its efficacy largely on the receptivity of the community at large, a public hearing is called for. This may be painful; extreme views on both sides are sure to be loudly proclaimed, but the alternative is to ignore the community entirely. Surely the history of the last five years teaches the lack of wisdom in that course.

Under no circumstances should the re-submission of the project to the Board of Estimate be framed so as to permit the killing of the entire project! I believe it is entirely possible to present to the Board a tandem proposition that would replace the present plan and project only if the new one is adopted.

Of course these legal determinations are properly within the province of the Corporation Counsel whose opinion on all aspects of this proposal will necessarily be required.

While on a clean slate, in another area, free from the excruciating complexities that have twisted the Forest Hills situation into the distortion it has become, I might favor the mix approach, I do not favor it here. In my judgment the critical factors here are the size, and the number of units which will be utilized for low income families. Many are convinced—and there is evidence to support the point of view—that if a mix is agreed upon initially, those units may eventually be converted largely into low income housing. That danger is heightened by the unique circumstances affecting the Forest Hills project. It is reasonable to believe that middle income housing on this site might not be generally attractive to the ordinary market in view of the project's spectacular history. Thus, given the premise that approximately 430 units are the minimum needed and the maximum tolerable, it would simply complicate the situation to increase the physical size of the project in order to add middle income units. In addition to presenting the threat that these units might eventually be converted into low income, it would also proportionately fail to meet a number of the other complaints, such as scale and the excessive strain of supporting services. Thus, in order to provide a significant amount of middle income housing in addition to approximately 430 low-income units, the project would have to consist of three buildings each a minimum of 18 to 20 stories. I would regard that as excessive.

Supplemental Recommendations

Without respect to whether the project proceeds as originally planned or in some modified version, there are some steps which I would recommend as almost unarguably helpful:

1. There is no question that when all the decisions as to form, height and composition have finally been made, problems will remain. Some tension and anxiety will persist although subdued in tone and extent. It will be essential that the entire City make every effort to assure the success of the endeavor for everyone's sake: for its occupants, who are the principal concern of the entire enterprise, for the immediately surrounding community and for the City at large. Every form of supplemental assistance must be brought to bear and in the process the Forest Hills community itself should be intimately involved. I am pleased to report that many private organizations and individuals have come forward in recognition of this need and have offered their full assistance and cooperation. Three groups particularly, have embodied their willingness to participate in well reasoned and meaningful programs and commitments. Thus, the American Jewish Committee has specifically committed itself to join in a consortium involving representatives from the project, the private sector, including Forest Hills residents, and government at all levels. The consortium would seek governmental and private funding for special programs and projects designed to aid the project's tenants. The A.J.C. has agreed to assign a full time staff to organize and coordinate this effort at its own expense. Among its goals would be the hiring of expert consultants and the initiation of special programs for the tenants in such highly useful areas as vocational training, employment, counselling, geriatric programs and services, social welfare, health services, pre-school and adult educational programs, safety and security studies, child and health care programs and recreation activities. The consortium would involve specialized voluntary agencies such as Catholic and Protestant Charities and J.A.S.A. The American Jewish Congress has also come forward with a program designed to assure that the project receive the benefit of the fullest possible police, transportation, educational and other facilities. In previous discussions with Chairman Golar, agreement was reached as to the details of this program. The Forest Hills Neighbors, a corporation consisting of more than 100 dues-paying residents of the area, has designed a program aimed at the same objectives. I regard this latter group's efforts as worthy of special note since it is an organization comprised exclusively of residents of the affected community. Other groups and individuals have also indicated their willingness to serve in this effort; notable among them are the Anti-Defamation League and Queens Council B'nai B'rith.

It is a good, helpful and perhaps even inspiring sign that so many are prepared to join meaningfully with the project's tenants in the effort to make this project work. These groups, it seems to me, deserve the fullest encouragement and cooperation of the City; it should be afforded them tangibly and immediately. I would recommend that regardless of any other action that may be taken as a result of this report, as soon as possible you appoint a member of your staff to serve as a coordinator whose function it will be to draw together these groups and to put their proposed programs into operation without delay. It would be unfortunate if by inadvertence or indifference this show of enthusiasm and substantial promise of intelligent assistance should be permitted to dissipate. The goals of these three groups and the others I have spoken to are totally compatible. Given their obvious good will there should be no problem in melding them together into a concerted and efficient effort. (The proposals are attached hereto as "Addendum B").

2. "Blockbusting" looms as an obvious problem particularly in light of the nature of the public debate over the past several months. The danger that parasitical exploiters may attempt to capitalize on the fears of some residents should be dealt with immediately. I would recommend that you call upon Secretary of State Lomenzo and City Human Rights Commission Chairman Norton to use the full force of the law and facilities at their command to protect the Forest Hills community (and ultimately the project tenants) against such activity.

3. The massive, agonizing and complex housing problems that oppress Chairman Golar and the entire City require, it seems to me, a totally new look at the housing laws and policies. One aspect of the overall situation which I regard as worthy of particular note has to do with the necessity for a regional approach to the housing problem. As long as suburban areas surrounding our City refuse to carry their fair share of the burden of low-income people and drive them back out of necessity into the core City, the problem may remain insoluble. The legal principle that mandates the building of scatter site housing in New York City should operate as fully in the suburbs. The State and Federal governments, which have primary jurisdiction in this area, ought to be called upon to act as aggressively as possible to assure a full application of the Federal constitutional law to the suburbs. Newspaper accounts as recent as this last week-end pointed out that H.U.D. has insisted on compliance in one of our neighboring suburban counties. If the reports were accurate, the attitude of that county's governmental officials was that they would rather surrender their full housing allocations than meet the legal obligation. If that is indeed the case then conceivably the City, which has chosen to meet its obligations, may profit from a re-distribution of housing funds away from those suburbs and into this area of greater need. The tools are at hand;

administration guidelines may be fully enforced; lawsuits may be brought. The results apparently would be either a proliferation of low income housing in middle income suburban areas, thereby reducing some of the burden on the City, or a larger share of the available housing monies for the City. In either case there is everything to be gained and nothing to be lost.

4. Since I regard the Section 23 approach to dispersal of low-income families in middle income areas as a theoretically superior device for achieving the objectives of scatter site housing, I would recommend that everything possible be done to make that approach a more practically useful tool. This would probably require at least two things, an increase in the Federal limits on the amount of monthly rent that will qualify, and more importantly some method for inducing landlords in middle income areas to make apartments available. This may be impossible; certainly it cannot be done easily. Many in the real estate industry regard any attempt at economic integration as pointless. Owners of flourishing apartment house developments in middle income white areas of Queens have little incentive to introduce low-income tenants who might be "disruptive." On the other hand there is no reason why some concerted attempt should not be made to reach the real estate industry and to discuss the matter jointly with them, no matter how unlikely the chance for success. It is at least conceivable that ways may be found, perhaps by agreements as to screening and possible tax abatements, which may be productive.

5. No one could make an in-depth study of the Forest Hills situation without being struck by the question raised as to the proper mechanics for obtaining helpful community participation. Total local community control is neither feasible nor desirable. On the other hand better means for communication with affected neighborhoods than were utilized in the Forest Hills situation must be found. Helpful steps have been taken in the last five years; Community Boards which were only emerging in 1966 have—thanks to the hard work of scores of Community Board Chairmen and members—become useful tools. But much more can be done along these lines. Board powers can be expanded and their ability to reflect accurately the consensus of their communities can be enhanced. Although I have offered the City a number of suggestions along these lines in the past, I hesitate to report them now because of the imminence of the Charter Revision Commission, whose function it will be to consider this problem among others, in a broad inquiry into our entire governmental structure. I would urge you to make special note of the Forest Hills experience in your dealings with this Commission. In this connection I

attach as "Addendum C" a brief statement by Commissioner Martin Gallent of the City Planning Commission describing a proposal for selecting scatter sites on a city-wide allocation basis. From what I have learned I believe Commissioner Gallent's approach to be worth serious consideration. It too, however, will depend largely upon the form of governmental structure that emerges from the Charter Revision Commission's deliberations.

THE IMMEDIATE FUTURE OF LOW-INCOME HOUSING IN QUEENS

No matter what the eventual size of the Forest Hills project, it will leave a great deal more to be done. Hundreds of thousands of low-income people are living in sub-standard and in some cases uncivilized conditions. There is a moral obligation to provide them with suitable dwellings and an opportunity to improve themselves. For the most part the City has sought to meet this need by providing new structures in the midst of the deterioration. That approach in various forms continues—and will apparently continue indefinitely. As noted earlier, however, it seems to me inescapable that in attempting to meet the obligation to provide integrated housing opportunities, we must, for the time being at least, also continue to build projects in middle income areas. The use of Section 23 and the mix approach should continue and, if possible, be enhanced. To the extent these methods become significant they will reduce the need for projects, but for now the City is obliged to build projects outside of ghetto areas. That effort, I suspect, may be doomed unless the lessons of Forest Hills are heeded. It would seem to me that at the minimum:

1. The sites selected must be distributed throughout Queens, preferably in areas of different ethnic and religious composition. Whatever burden is involved in the acceptance of scatter site projects should be spread as equitably as possible across the County.

2. Sites must be selected only after the fullest possible community input, making generous use of the present Community Boards and whatever other vehicles are available.

3. In the selection of sites, Commissioner Gallent's concept, involving the allocation of a specific number of units to a general area with the decision as to precise location being left to the community, should be carefully considered.

4. The scale and dimensions of the project should be kept as small as possible. This would be made easier by an adjustment in the Federal guidelines. While the determination as to a suitable size must be made *ad hoc*, the desideratum is clear: effective scatter site depends upon a melding of

the project with the surrounding community; form and size which tend to unduly distinguish and identify the project structures should be avoided.

5. Wherever possible supporting services should be enhanced and beefed up before, or simultaneously with, the development of the project.

6. In all cases consortiums similar to the one planned for Forest Hills should be encouraged and assisted.

7. The actual planning of projects within the guidelines suggested above should begin immediately. The need for units increases daily; they should be provided as soon as possible. Conceivably, specific sites might have been found in the course of this investigation and announced in this report. To have done so would have been to violate one of the principles that emerges from the Forest Hills experience; the necessity for community involvement in advance of the decision to move forward in a given location. I can report to you that I discussed this matter with Boro President Manes and he agrees provision must be made as soon as possible for the placing of additional units in Queens County. There appears to be no reason why Chairman Golar and the Boro President cannot commence their planning at once.

CONCLUDING NOTE

Housing is clearly not the answer to the poverty dilemma. The answer lies in education, jobs, security and acceptance. The poor cannot be moved up the social ladder simply by depositing them in new housing or even new environments; their basic problems will not be solved by osmosis. At the very most, scatter site housing may help, but if its proponents make the mistake of regarding it as a total, or even substantial, solution they risk obscuring the greater needs.

On the other hand, while pursuing the elusive answers to the radical problems, the City must use whatever partial remedies are immediately available, however inadequate they appear to be. As a matter of plain legal and moral obligation to thousands of low-income families, housing must be provided and it must be provided on an integrated basis. The only devices available to do this are at best imperfect, but they must be utilized for what they are worth. These devices should be re-studied and improved, but we cannot afford the luxury of doing nothing while we are waiting to find a way of doing everything.

I have suggested revisions in the project because I believe that these revisions would benefit not only the community but the tenants and the City itself. I believe they are true to the great need which inspired the project in the first place while at the same time they would sufficiently obviate defects inherent in the project as originally proposed so as to provide a greater assurance of its success. I believe that to permit the project to go forward as planned may be to jeopardize scatter site housing in this city for many years to come. The reduction of 408 units now may assure many times that number of units in the near future.

The suggestions set forth in this report will produce controversy. To some extent the opinions are predictable. I have already been contacted by some who, even before reading the report, indicated they will object vehemently to any recommendation that does not coincide totally with their polar points of view.

It seems to me it is easier to take one of the extreme positions—for or against the entire project exactly as it is. There is a tendency to regard the fiercely articulated, simple, extreme posture as the more courageous one. It has the advantage too, of assuring the concurrence at least of those on one side of the controversy. To me these are easier positions to take because they avoid many of the subtleties and exquisitely balanced conflicts that merge to make this situation the conundrum it is. I have been driven to the middle position not out of a desire to seek shelter, but by the inexorable crosscurrents of closely matched competing considerations.

The position I recommend will call for political courage on the part of those who assume it, since criticism and pressure from both sides is inevitable. Hopefully, however, the criticism will be outweighed by a predominant reasonableness which recognizes and appreciates what was stated by a great man long ago:

> "All government—indeed, every human benefit and enjoyment, every virtue and every prudent act—is founded on compromise. . . ." EDMUND BURKE
> *Speech on conciliation with America, March 22, 1775*

Respectfully submitted,
MARIO MATTHEW CUOMO
July 25, 1972

ADDENDUM A

COST ANALYSIS FOR FOREST HILLS PROJECT

7/12/72 Revised 7/18/72

Building Elevation	24 Stories	22 Stories	20 Stories	18 Stories	16 Stories	14 Stories	12 Stories	Two 18 Story Buildings
No. of Dwelling Units (Total/Elderly)	840/341	792/330	720/300	648/270	576/240	504/210	432/180	432/180
Total Development Cost (incl. air cond.)	$31,240,000	$30,530,582	$29,551,840	$28,787,231	$27,017,507	$25,416,883	$23,755,897	$23,750,000
110% of Prototype Limits	23,474,000	21,877,680	19,888,800	17,899,921	15,911,040	13,922,160	11,933,280	11,933,280
D. C. & E. (1460, 1465 & cont.)	21,390,216	20,538,200	19,600,900	18,887,357	17,228,810	15,828,810	14,344,810	14,460,000
Equity Contribution by the City	—	—	—	987,436	1,317,770	1,906,640	2,411,550	2,527,000
Cost Per Dwelling Unit	$37,172	$38,547	$41,043	$44,427	$46,905	$50,428	$54,970	$54,970
Units Deleted Total/Elderly	—	48/11	120/41	192/72	264/101	336/131	408/161	408/161

NOTE: These figures assume floor deletions commencing with the ground floor levels and proceeding upward to typical floors.

FOREST HILLS NEIGHBORS
P.O. BOX 102
FOREST HILLS, N.Y. 11375

June 28, 1972

MR. MARIO CUOMO
32 Court Street
Brooklyn, New York 11201

Dear Mario:

It was pleasant meeting with you the other day. The diversity of personal opinions is representative of our membership and I hope you agree that this is a strength in dealing with the community at large. Given certain conditions our numbers will grow and a couple of years from now Forest Hills will have a much different image from the one which has been projected the past few months. Don't be cynical!

We're novices at submitting formal proposals so I'd like this letter to serve as the vehicle for transmitting our suggestions. Leave your blue pencil aside as I'd like you to incorporate this data as wholly as possible into your report.

Without being preachy let me emphasize that it is crucial for the Administration to approach the resolution of the conflict with the view that the unusualness of the situation demands unusual action. Until this is acknowledged, it is doubtful much meaningful progress can be made. As I expressed the other evening, any contemplated change in structure or tenant composition does not make for success of the project. It is my view that those individuals and groups who have injected themselves into the controversy, both for and against the project, will claim some sort of victory and then go elsewhere. The community residents who are frightened by the prospect of the project may breathe a momentary sigh of relief. And then we will be left with a situation where a community's rawest emotions have been stirred and now abandoned. In this vacuum Forest Hills Neighbors will have to work. Without the sensitive cooperation of the Administration it will be a struggle which, quite candidly, I'm not sure we can handle. Therefore, I urge upon you very serious consideration of the ideas I present below.

As I see it, the process must be divided into two stages. The first relates to steps which must be taken immediately to prepare the community and the second concerns itself with the planning of actual programs which will go into effect once the tenants start moving in. Let me list some suggestions for Stage I.

PREPARING THE COMMUNITY

1. Converting Project Into Low-Income Co-op to be Managed by a Private Concern

Governmental credibility and public attitudes are the keys here. Whether true or not, most people believe that people who own their own homes or live in Co-ops take better care of the property. By such a move we are off the issue of anti-social behavior of low-income tenants. Second, we have removed the cloud of disbelief over governmental statements of proper maintenance. Third, we instill a sense of pride in the project's tenants thus helping to develop a greater desire to become part of the community.

2. Hiring of Private Firm to Plan and Execute Continuing Public Relations Campaign

A professional public relations firm accustomed to selling ideas, can be instrumental in turning the situation around. Myths must be debunked; things must be put into perspective. A PR outfit can shed light on conditions in Forest Hills today—age, income, etc.—thus destroying erroneous views of affluence and current shortages of facilities. They must also humanize the profile of a low-income housing tenant through a continuing series of human interest stories in the media about who lives in low-income projects, who's on welfare, what kinds of creative activities do project tenants participate in in other projects around the city. Are all projects alike? If not, why not? These are merely suggestions to illustrate the kind of careful planning which must take place.

3. Involvement of Tenants

Once tenants are selected, perhaps they can cooperate in a constructive manner which I'll put under the banner of community relations. Certainly the creation of a strong tenants association must be fostered. Bring them into contact with the community prior to their moving in. That means having them as speakers before local community organizations. It means publicizing who they are. It means putting them in touch with Parents Associations so a dialogue can begin immediately. Perhaps innovative programs are necessary to absorb the new children as opposed to merely stuffing the children from the project into existing structures.

Now let me move to Stage II.

PROGRAMS AND SERVICES TO BE PROVIDED

1. Child Care Center

This deserves highest priority since it will serve as a rallying point for people on all sides of the conflict. It will also be the first one in the community. As such it must be as attractive and enticing as possible. It is crucial that space be provided on the site to accommodate the number of pre-elementary school age children who will live in the development as well as an equal number who live in the surrounding community. This center should enjoy the joint sponsorship of several private non-profit organizations which the entire Forest Hills community respects. There should also be an affiliation with the Bank Street School of Education or Queens College. Teenagers as well as elderly people living in the project can be utilized in various aspects of the Center. As part of this program, facilities and funds must be allocated for the development of an exciting teenage program.

2. Health Care

Facilities must be provided to meet the health needs of all tenants. Questions such as psychiatric social workers, visiting nurse and home-maker services, continuing family care at a price which tenants can afford are some of the areas where the Administration can enlist the aid of existing non-profit agencies to become involved.

3. Orientation Program for Tenants

A program should be developed to acquaint tenants with community services and facilities.

4. Cultural Events

Exciting events, similar to the Schaefer Music Festival in Central Park, should be held on the grounds of the project. The intent here is to bring community residents into the project as often as possible.

5. High School

The Administration must proceed as rapidly as possible with the construction of New Queens High School in Corona.

6. Physical Structure

The following items should be part of the buildings: (a) 24-hour security guards, (b) buzzer system or closed circuit TV, (c) superintendent should live on the premises. In this category, we are saying that of all the features now known to exist in City housing projects, those which are the best should be included here.

May I emphasize, Mario, that it is important for the Administration to begin dialogues with existing private organizations. Many of them have contacted me and wish to be of help. Essentially they are asking what we would like them to do. Well, with a comprehensive, coordinated program, I think there is much they can do. And the Administration can spearhead the effort. All of this, of course, must be soundly publicized so the community can begin to read and see constructive efforts being put forth.

And let me add one further point. I think it would be helpful if a key civil servant in each of the appropriate city agencies were given the responsibility of beginning to talk with community organizations—in and out of Forest Hills—in terms of a mutual effort. These civil servants must spend their time almost exclusively on Forest Hills until such time as the community attitude becomes one of receptive response. The naming of a civil servant will assure the continuity of the program beyond the next Mayoralty election, thus giving Forest Hills residents some degree of assurance that commitments made by the current administration will be continued with the next one, way after the headlines stop featuring Forest Hills.

Well, there you have it. Hopefully, it will serve some good. If you want to discuss any particular point, please get in touch.

Cordially,
PAUL SANDMAN
President

PUBLIC HOUSING AND THE LOCAL PLANNING BOARDS

Planning for housing at this time requires that we evaluate any proposal in terms of at least the following criteria:

1. Relocation load and available facilities.
2. Availability of financing and cost criteria.
3. Impact on community infrastructure.
4. Social impact.
5. Capital budget consequences.
   a) capital improvement plan.
   b) special funds and available sources.
6. Sponsorship, builder, etc.
7. Government policy regarding existing laws and quality of opportunity.

Assuming the above as essential criteria, how can the City best proceed to implement a policy of providing housing for the disadvantaged and the poor?

It seems apparent that the present direction of public housing is toward meaningful decentralization, or small scale scatter site housing with strong community involvement.

One possible means of achieving this goal is by involving local planning boards, of which there are 62 in New York City.

Local planning boards are mandated by New York City Charter, despite the existence in almost every area of the City of civic organizations. The original concept was to involve the diverse communities of the City in the planning process for their own community. They have performed their function with varying degrees of success. Some have been outstanding;

some abject failures. Some board members see their function as super civic organizations whose existence is predicated on their mirroring only the views of their community as they see it. Others have given time, effort and energy to develop new concepts, suggesting imaginative alternatives and working with the borough offices of the Department of City Planning for effective change and strengthening of their community. Other board members see themselves in a total political role and are often negative, or hostile to change or planning, refusing to see City-wide problems and their role in any solutions.

Community Planning Boards nevertheless are popular organizations to which citizens want to join, and upon becoming members, are reluctant to leave. They have become an important part of the planning process where they utilize their initiative and are willing to understand the scope and difficulty of the City's resources and problems.

An integral part of the planning process is to be willing to plan for all of the people, including the poor. Although the poor may not be located in each of the 62 planning board areas, the need to scatter housing facilities and opportunities throughout the region and therefore throughout the City, is essential. *Large, massive housing for the poor and disadvantaged is counter-productive.* Locating housing throughout the City (in 62 planning board areas) in scale with the area, taking into consideration the local infrastructure of the areas, is both desirable, necessary and, in fact, a Federal mandate.

Involving the 62 local planning boards in developing a public housing strategy, has, of course, its many difficulties, but I am convinced that they can and will meaningfully participate. I, therefore, suggest that each of the 62 local planning boards assist in planning and development of 150 to 250 units of public housing in their respective districts over a three year period. This will then provide the City with 9,300 to 15,500 units.

Before such a program could be implemented, it is essential that the City Planning Commission analyze each of the planning areas to determine housing feasibility in each of the 62 districts, taking into account demographic statistics, open space, schools, health facilities, shopping, transportation, etc. Where special problems arise, alternative suggestion should be outlined.

In any such analysis, certain planning districts will be judged unsuitable for additional public housing, having a disproportionate number of public housing units. In such districts, suggestions and incentives for other types of housing could be explored with the board. Where, however, public housing is judged to be appropriate, the local board should play an integral part in locating the site for these units, determining the mix of family and elderly apartments and the type of units such as the number of rooms, design review, including height and coverage. *Most important, the board should be involved in implementing guidelines for tenant selection.* No community group or any local planning board should be involved in the actual tenant selection, but rather, once the guidelines for tenant selection are established, the local planning board could insure that these guidelines and criteria are adhered to. There are, of course, Federal criteria to determine eligibility for public housing and some modification of these criteria may be necessary to accommodate this program.

No lay group can be expected to do a constructive planning job without expert assistance and guidance. The fine job that the borough offices of the Department of City Planning has been doing must be expanded and the Housing Authority and the Borough President's Offices should provide increased technical assistance to the boards. Information concerning school utilization, health services, sewers, water mains and environmental questions, should be provided and considered as a part of the local planning operation.

These boards should also have the option, where appropriate, and where possible, to provide different types of public housing, such as rent supplements, 20 to 30% low-income in Mitchell Lama housing, Turnkey III, as well as other strategies.

Housing planned in urban renewal, model city areas, and in those units now in the planning process, would not be counted as part of the 150 to 250 units.

This plan presupposes a vital role for the Federal Government. Additional assistance must be made available from Washington to assist communities where the local board assumes its responsibility. Funds should be made available through the City to these areas for needed parks, sewers and special school programs, etc. Boards that do not accept their responsibility retain their right and prerogative to articulate their objections and the City retains its mandate to plan in default of the local board.

Where special opportunity areas exist for the City, such as South Richmond, the City, of course, retains its mandate to continue overall planning in cooperation with the local board.

The criteria enumerated at the beginning of this article do not mitigate against the proposal, but rather will facilitate a meaningful, scatter site public housing program.

Local boards have already been provided with initial statistical information, detailed maps, a history of their area, etc., in the Proposal for the Master Plan for New York City. The people of this City, the local planning boards, and the City government now have the opportunity to actually create the plan for the City.

MARTIN GALLENT